SURVIVING

A Guide for Victims, Families, Friends and Professionals

Allison Brittsan
Clarene Shelley

Word Services, Inc.
Lakewood, Colorado

Copyright © 1994 by Allison Brittsan and Clarene Shelley

Published by:

Word Services, Inc.
2610 S. Miller Drive, #101
Lakewood, CO 80227

Cataloging in Publication Data

Brittsan, Allison Arthur.

Surviving: A guide for victims, families, friends and professionals
/Allison Brittsan and Clarene Shelley.
p. 192 cm.
Includes bibliography.
1. Victim assistance   2. Domestic violence/crime
I. Brittsan, Allison, 1953- . II. Shelley, Clarene, 1949-
III. Title
HV1431.J 1994   362.7
ISBN 0-9626437-4-2

Cover Design by E.P. Puffin & Co., Denver, CO.

Printed by Gilliland Printing, Inc., Arkansas City, KS.

ISBN Number: 0-9626437-4-2

Printed in the United States of America.

To all the victims the system failed

Chinese symbol for Crisis. It also means Opportunity.

SURVIVING:

A Guide for Victims, Families, Friends, and Professionals

TABLE OF CONTENTS

FOREWORD

In 1972 a brave young woman in St. Louis, Carol Vittert, realizing the shock, pain and frustration that victims suffer, became the founder of Aid for Victims of Crime, the first comprehensive victim service organization in the United States. Over the next decade, her realization was echoed through the establishment of victim assistance programs throughout the country. Those programs ranged from rape crisis centers, domestic violence shelters, survivors of homicide victims projects, victim/witness assistance programs, and other comprehensive service organizations.

As victimization increased and programs proliferated, victims and their advocates joined forces in a number of national organizations, including the National Organization for Victim Assistance, the National Coalition Against Sexual Assault, the National Coalition Against Domestic Violence, Mothers Against Drunk Driving, and Parents of Murdered Children. The first decade of the victims' movement culminated in the creation of the 1982 President's Task Force on Victims of Crime.

More than twenty years after Carol Vittert's epiphany, the achievements of the movement are reflected not only in nearly 10,000 programs but also in legislated rights for victims within the criminal justice system in all fifty states. In addition, counselors and advocates have learned that victims of crime are similar to other victims of crisis. Many victim assistance professionals are now responding to community tragedies of all types. The decade of the '90s promises to hold even more hope for victims with the new Violence Against Women Act, state constitutional amendments ensuring that rights are more than rhetoric, and increased funding for services to victims of all trauma.

Despite such progress, however, most people still feel helpless when victimization strikes them or their loved ones. They don't know what to do or what to say. And, often they don't know where to turn for help. *Surviving: A Guide for Victims, Families, Friends, and Professionals* is a good primer for people who care about victims. It serves as a helpful reference for victims and their loved ones and a basic text for professionals in the victim assistance field. Being aware of common reactions to victimization can mitigate the long-term effects of trauma.

Allison Brittsan and Clarene Shelley have struck a nice chord in their effort to provide complex information in practical and readable terms. Their book is written clearly and concisely. It highlights the most important reactions that typify unique victimization experiences and outlines suggested responses.

There are two important differences between this book and others in this field. The first is that it addresses most types of victimization, including accident victims, families of victims of sudden death, and victims of natural and man-made disasters. In doing this, the book recognizes the common bond of victimization while acknowledging the differences between these victims and victims of various types of crime.

The second difference is that the book is jointly authored by a victim-assistance counselor and a law enforcement officer. This partnership sets the tone for one of the book's messages: that the best response to victimization is one of teamwork between the criminal-justice system, victim service workers, and other sources of social support, such as family or friends. Teamwork is critical in meeting the needs and ensuring the rights of victims.

FOREWORD

Surviving the trauma of victimization is never easy, but the information in this book can help people understand better some of the elements of that survival.

Marlene A. Young
Executive Director
National Organization for Victim Assistance
January 1994

PREFACE

During the course of our careers in victim advocacy and law enforcement, we have seen successes and failures in helping victims cope with the effects of their victimization. We hope that the information in this book will empower victims to become survivors, encourage the people who care about them to intervene in ways that do not re-victimize, and educate professionals and clergy in the trauma and reactions associated with various types of victimization.

Whether or not a victim becomes involved in the criminal justice system, it is imperative that anyone who knows of his or her trauma understand the range of potential reactions to crisis and respond appropriately. We have learned from experience that it is the support given to victims by other people in their lives that ultimately encourages them to be winners. It is hoped that this book becomes a valuable tool to help you deal with victimization, no matter what your role.

Allison Brittsan
Clarene Shelley
Lakewood, Colorado

ACKNOWLEDGMENTS

I am grateful to the following people who have influenced, supported and helped me in my work with victims: Jeff Kendig, Frances Cosby, Nancy Rich, Dr. Richard Spiegle, and the many dedicated, caring police officers, district attorneys, victim advocates, and others. My co-author, Clarene Shelley—whose personal and professional relationship I deeply value—my husband, Dan, children, Melanie and Matthew, have provided the support and encouragement that made this dream a reality. The guidance and insights of Charlotte Meares and Ben McDonald have enhanced the clarity and focus of *Surviving*.

Allison Brittsan

This book is possible only because every victim I have come to know during my career has taught me something, contributing to my understanding of and sensitivity for the issues each faces. I wish to thank Dora Marcus and Candy Gaboriault for their time and helpful suggestions, as well as Nancy and Bill Astor for their prayerful support. My daughter, Jan, convinced me this book was needed and, just as important, that it was possible. For their ideas and diligent work, I want to thank Ben McDonald and Charlotte Meares. To Allison Brittsan, my co-author and frequent workshop teammate, whose caring professionalism I deeply respect, and to all the many unnamed influences in my life who helped make this book possible, thank you.

Clarene Shelley

The authors have made every effort to avoid sexist language in this book and to present this material in a way that does not discriminate on the basis of race, age or sex. However, to avoid repeated and awkward "he or she" constructions in the text, either the male or female pronoun has been used in most instances. Such use of male gender over female does not imply exclusivity for that reference.

INTRODUCTION

Maurine fidgeted. Balancing Laura's favorite cake in her left hand, she pressed her index finger against the back door bell for the third time. Again she waited, then cupped her free hand between the glass and her forehead, searching past her reflection and the children's fingerprints for her friend.

"Oh no, dear God, no," she whispered. "Not again."

The storm door slammed behind her with a loud, metallic clap, and the silhouette slumped against the refrigerator shuddered. Maurine dropped to her knees and drew the trembling figure into her arms. Laura winced in pain, then stared vacantly across her brightly polished floor.

"I fell," she lied. Her words echoed staccato, brittle. The broad, blue bruise from her left cheek bone to her jaw glistened wet. Small red beads of blood had already congealed on her split lip.

Maurine had no idea how, or if, she could protect Laura from her husband's beatings. She only knew she had to try.

Surviving, A Guide for Victims, Families, Friends, and Professionals is for Maurine, Laura and anyone who is a victim or who cares about a victim. *Surviving* offers clear, concise answers to tough questions asked by those experiencing crisis and those responding to one. In the following chapters, we will call these helpers "caregivers" and "first-responders."

The real heroes in any crisis, say these dedicated caregivers, are the women, men, and children who overcome the adversity of victimization and begin their lives again, stronger, wiser, and better prepared to meet the challenges of the future.

Every effective victim advocate brings to the intervention process skills that can't be taught—intuition, sensitivity—as well as those that can—communication dynamics. Insightfully, they recognize that the human potential leaves plenty of space for infinite reactions to events in life. Caregivers' questions—"What should I say?" "What should I do?" "How can I best help someone who needs intervention NOW?" "How do I recognize victimization when there is no visible injury?"—do not discount their intuitive responses, their instinctual protective capabilities, but reflect, instead, their desire to clearly understand specific reactions by victims to specific stressors and learn appropriate responses that lead the victim to the path of survival.

Surviving answers these questions and many more. While surveying various categories of crisis, *Surviving* focuses on three primary goals, to:

- Ease the pain of victimization

- Mobilize resources to assist victims and survivors

- Empower victims and survivors to regain balance, or equilibrium

Each of these goals is achieved through intervention. But as we have intimated, effective intervention is grounded in awareness and observation of the physical, emotional, financial, and other burdens placed on individuals by their various crises.

This is not a first-aid "how-to" book. Medical emergencies are, indeed, a very real and often primary component of victimization that caregivers and first-responders must know how to assess. However, it is beyond the scope and intent of *Surviving* to provide instruction in emergency medical care. Many excellent resources and community programs offer instruction and certification in first-aid and life-saving.

Step-by-step, *Surviving* walks anyone encountering a victim situation through the intervention process. It is designed to supplement professional training as well as to provide non-professional first-responders with the skills necessary to recognize trauma reactions, the stages of recovery, and the opportunities to promote and support healing.

Chapter I introduces the concept of stress, its relationship to crisis development, general categories of crisis, and misconceptions surrounding victimization.

Chapter II explores pathways for coping with crisis, from the standpoint of victim as well as from that of caregiver or first-responder. Clear guidelines enhance personal experience and training for lay-helpers and professionals alike so that they may enable victims and loved ones to meet the challenges of survival.

Chapter III examines some of the bureaucratic stumbling blocks, fine print, and red tape that hinder effective victim advocacy. We believe that basic knowledge of the criminal justice system enables victims, first-responders, friends, and family to mobilize its power on their behalf and opens the doors to legislation for equitable treatment.

Successive chapters detail potential reactions to specific categories of victimization, such as domestic violence, sexual assault, assault and robbery, sudden death, disasters, as well as elderly and child abuse and neglect situations. In every instance, we have outlined empowering strategies for both first-responders and victims themselves. Actual case histories (victims' names and specific details have been changed to protect their privacy) are included to achieve several objectives. They provide insights into victims' emotional turmoil, demonstrate victim-responder interactions, and map avenues for affecting change.

The American Medical Association has made the plight of the battered woman one of its national priorities. Chapter IV on domestic violence sheds light on the battering cycle, which traps victims in patterns of repeated abuse. Included is a risk factor checklist that can be used to assess if the victim is in danger.

Second only to homicide, rape has been recognized as the most heinous of crimes. Its long-term emotional effects depend both on the victim and the early support she receives. Of course, not every victim of rape is female, but women and girls far and away comprise the majority of victims. Socio-cultural influences bear heavily on the impact rape is likely to have on either sex.

By increasing public awareness regarding the vast number of unreported and unsuccessfully prosecuted cases of rape, we hope to garner greater protection for potential victims as well as fair treatment and comprehensive resources for those who have been victimized. As acquaintance/date rape receives increasing national attention, we are encouraged that communities are taking steps to ensure the safety of all its female citizens. Such protective measures can also be effective for special groups of individuals vulnerable to rape, such as the physically or mentally challenged, children, and the elderly.

Chapter V includes guidelines for conducting effective interviews with victims of rape and emphasizes sensitivity to victims and treating them with dignity and respect.

Incidents of assault and robbery can be devastating, even debilitating, for victims who are injured both physically—including near-death experiences—and emotionally. Reminders of their trauma may be slow to fade and may rekindle fear and anger. Chapter VI explains why first-responders, caregivers and professionals must suspend judgment about victims' complicity in risk associated with their victimization in order to understand the complexity of the crime paradigm.

Chapter VII, "Losing a Loved One to Sudden Death," reveals how surviving family members and friends, confronted by the sudden death of someone close to them, can themselves become victims. Discussed are homicide, sudden natural death, suicide, and sudden infant death syndrome, or SIDS.

Tomorrow's child faces potential disasters unimagined by her grandparents. Chapter VIII discusses the impact of both natural disasters and man-made catastrophic events: crises wrought by intentional and negligent acts, conflict, and even out-of-control technology. Caregivers and first-responders who understand how the psyche deals with such monumental blows to innate order and tranquility can facilitate victims' recovery by helping them discover new coping strategies and re-establish control.

When the victim advocate walks into unfamiliar territory or when additional resources are necessary to help the victim achieve balance and equilibrium, help is available. The Appendix provides referral information for most types of crisis and tips for locating community, state, and federal agencies specializing in crime victim compensation, as well as legal, medical, and emotional assistance.

In the early 1980s, President Ronald Reagan initiated the President's Task Force on Victims of Crime. After extensive hearings and testimony, this commission concluded that victims were consistently ignored, mistreated, blamed, and accorded little or no respect. It determined that victims' experiences with the criminal justice system had been that of "re-victimization," which had an unfortunate chilling-effect on their willingness to become involved in criminal prosecution.

Recognizing this, the President's Task Force in 1983 filed a comprehensive report containing 68 specific recommendations. The most significant recommendation enacted to date is the federal Victims of Crime Act (VOCA) that assists states in providing services and compensatory funds to victims of crime.

Victims' advocates initiated a federal constitutional amendment to accord victims of crimes specific rights. Before this can take place, however, 37 states must first ratify their own constitutional amendments supporting victim advocacy. As of this printing, 13 states have done just that. These amendments and related legislation are presently constructed both to protect victims of crime and provide them with remedial or compensatory services. Such bold actions have resulted in far-reaching reform on state levels and promise greater equity for those brought into the criminal justice system.

Is all this reform really necessary? Since those tumultuous days when our forefathers framed our noble constitution, the Supreme Court has interpreted personal liberty so broadly as to protect the accused at the expense of his victim, ironically imposing undue hardship and injustice on innocents. Today, child and elderly victims, those with disabilities, and immediate family may be eligible for crisis intervention, victim compensation, financial assistance, victim assistance, as well as legal, mental health, rehabilitative, transportation, translation, child care, and medical resources.

State law enforcement agencies are expeditiously responding to local Crime Victim Rights Amendments by assuring that victims are notified of all their rights and are treated with fairness, respect, and dignity. In addition, many state law enforcement agencies are participating in and making available to victims specific community resources to alleviate the burden historically placed upon them.

For information regarding specific enabling legislation, victim advocates should contact their local Victims Assistance Coordinator. With the appropriate support, victims and survivors can cut through the confusion to recognize their choices and make informed decisions from a spectrum of viable alternatives.

For victims, families, and friends, *Surviving* becomes a manual for self-preservation, self-confidence, and self-integration. For survivors, it is reassurance that they, too, are not without support.

As a reference for first-responders, *Surviving* offers helpful techniques for shifting passivity to activity, acknowledging the emotional and physical investment of these dedicated people in the victim/survivor healing process.

Above all, we hope that *Surviving* empowers victims and survivors to liberate themselves from unnecessary pain and hardship.

Surviving is a process. Its meaning must embody the essence of living, an esoteric yet vital concept that distinguishes mere existence from life that is full, rich, and rewarding.

Because the journey from victim to victor can be long and arduous, we have marked places along the way where the weary will find rest, comfort, and encouragement. May your burden be lightened, traveler.

CHAPTER I

TYPES OF CRISIS AND TRAUMA

Crisis. It implies a sudden event for which an individual, family, or group is unprepared: a temporary upheaval of immediate and sometimes long-term impact. Crisis may refer to a personal, solitary occurrence, or an event that involves others.

Stress can precipitate crisis. Problems involving job, family, and health can increase stress and open the door to a crisis situation. So, too, can transitions in life: adolescence, marriage, divorce, retirement. We associate crisis with crimes, disasters, accidents, and unexpected deaths. And rightly so. In each case someone's life has been disrupted. Crises create victims.

Victim. It is a loosely cast noun preceded by run-together adjectives on the evening news: an accident victim; a homicide victim; a rape victim. In this context it refers to one who is "injured," or "destroyed." *Surviving, A Guide for Victims, Families, Friends, and Professionals* looks to the deeper meaning of victim: someone who is "sacrificed under any of various conditions, subjected to oppression, loss, suffering or mistreatment." Our concern is that when we have become desensitized to what it means and what it is like to be a victim, we have stepped over a dangerous threshold.

Victimization isn't selective or exclusive. There is no such thing as a victim profile. Victims are men, women, children of all races, ages, and economic levels.

People don't intentionally become victims. Thoughtless remarks, such as "they deserved what they got," inflict even greater injury on victims, who are usually ordinary people caught in what appear at the moment to be *extraordinary* situations.

Who causes someone to become a victim? Sometimes no one. Happenstance. Other times, one or more individuals are directly responsible for injury to another. The need to blame someone for their victimization is a natural adaptive reaction for victims. It can be healing, to a point. Victims blame the perpetrator, society, or themselves. Their friends and families may blame the victim, the "system," or each other. Blaming the victim, however, is always destructive and leads to deeper wounds that may never heal.

When we imply that their misery is of their own making, we have been insensitive to the feelings and experiences of victims. We assault them further with demeaning, degrading labels such as "patsy," "loser," "failure," or "sucker," which perpetuate misconceptions about victimization and do nothing to contribute to the healing process.

It is in trying to say and do the right things that we feel most deficient and inadequate. Yet, what is most necessary to help others is, to a great extent, already within us. We need only re-awaken our senses and rededicate ourselves to *common-unity*.

Past generations of Americans spent the years between birth and death denying their emotions. They had little time or tolerance for tears and self-pity. From their hard-work ethic came slogans as telling as, "Tough it out," "Put up or shut up," "Be a man." When the need arose, they met the challenges. With picks, shovels, and bleeding hands, they dug miners out of collapsed shafts, freed trapped residents from blazing tenements, and unearthed homesteads from mountains of sand.

Heroes still walk among us. Today, via remote control, we tune in to events a world away, zoom in on anguished faces, victims of bombings, massacres, earthquakes, fires: mourners weeping for husbands, sons, daughters, mothers.

We sympathize with their sorrow. It is easily seen and readily felt. Less visible and nearly unknown to us is the pain felt by our neighbors, friends, and family who have been tragically victimized by crime.

It is easiest to be compassionate toward the most vulnerable—children, the elderly, and handicapped—and least compassionate toward other victims whom we judge were in "the wrong place at the wrong time," or with whom we are most afraid to become involved. Victims of domestic violence, physical and sexual assault, or robbery make us aware of our own vulnerability, our unsafe surroundings, and our temporal existence.

To achieve the illusion of safety, we expend great time, money, and energy putting criminals out of sight and out of mind. But one problem doesn't go away. What happens to the objects of criminal behavior, the innocents whose lives have been disrupted? The time we take to know of them may be no more than a 40-second media bite.

In many crisis situations, a friend or family member is the first to intervene. His knowledge of the victim and the situation contributes to intervention efficacy. First-responders may also be untrained strangers who rely on experience and common sense for their approach to the victim. Professionals and paraprofessionals may have emergency medical training or counseling experience. Each of these helpers is presented with a unique challenge and opportunity: to reduce the long-term emotional effects on the victim of those critical first moments.

The psycho-physical human is a complex organism stimulated and influenced by internal and external stresses. Stress comes with living. While the type and severity of stress fluctuate, healthy individuals usually retain their equilibrium during peak stress times. When a minor crisis arises, they are able to cope with it. How well any individual copes—her reactions to severe stress, or crisis—is influenced by her experience and the number

11

and strength of current stressors that can weaken her defenses.

The human body responds to crisis physiologically and psychologically, or emotionally. Automatically and rapidly in time of danger, a burst of adrenaline prepares the body for "fight or flight." Heart rate increases. Breathing becomes more rapid. Involuntary sweating, vomiting, urination, or defecation may occur. This state of physical tension cannot be sustained for long, however, and eventually results in exhaustion.

During crisis, moods swing wildly. Victims can lose some or all of their ability to think or act coherently. They may be incapable of relating to others in normal ways.

The following stages are common to most persons experiencing crisis:

- Shock
- Denial
- Anger
- Frustration
- Grief
- Reconstruction, Equilibrium

Recent studies show that victims do not necessarily progress through these general stages in a clearly linear fashion. A stage may be skipped or repeated. Interestingly, the psychological stages of victims closely parallel those first identified by Elizabeth Kubler-Ross, known for her landmark studies on death and dying. Similarities can be readily understood in the context of the crisis event. For many victims, the crisis ordeal represents a symbolic death and, through healing, an opportunity for rebirth, or renewed life.

The impact of the crisis event often shatters the victim's illusion of security. Shock sets in. This stage may last a few hours to several days. In the next several stages, defense mechanisms, such as denial, take over. The mind may shunt the painful event out of recognition's range, or transform fear of the event to anger.

Directed outward anger becomes a positive force for movement and allows for the passage through grief. The victim may grieve the loss of a loved one, a lifestyle, possessions, self-confidence, self-determination, security, or a belief system. Processing this range of emotions may take from several days to several months.

In the final stage, which may require as little as a week or as much as several years, the victim's instinctive struggle to restore balance makes possible the goal— reconstruction. The victim orchestrates his newly gained knowledge and strength into self-empowerment.

Family, friends, and professionals who familiarize themselves with the spectrum of emotional reactions can be the victim's best defense against debilitating pain. Appropriate action can help victims set in place the mechanisms for affecting their own outcomes.

A first-responder, or caregiver, who is familiar with the individual's reaction to past crises can pass that useful information on to those who must assess how the person may act in a new situation. If the victimized person is usually calm or silent in the face of crisis, he will probably handle new stress in a similar manner. Conversely, if the person usually reacts hysterically to crises, or has a history of becoming paralyzed by fear, he is likely to continue that pattern.

A common response by caring people to anyone experiencing crisis is to "rescue." This book is not about rescuing, however. A more constructive intervention, especially during the critical impact stage, is interaction. Interaction isn't a "doing for," but a "working with." Interaction empowers the victim and enables him to re-weave his own safety net. From the very first, loved ones and strangers can do this by providing the victim with choices and alternatives for action.

This positive, control-taking behavior allows the victim to participate in decisions affecting his life and initiates

SURVIVING

the reconstruction process. When he takes the reins, he leaves dependence (brought on by need and confusion) behind. At the finish gate he discovers he has reintegrated his fragmented self.

In *Surviving,* seven categories of victims are discussed. They are:

- Domestic Violence
- Sexual Assault
- Assault and Robbery
- Survivors
- Disasters
- Elderly
- Children

DOMESTIC VIOLENCE

Domestic violence is a self-escalating, injurious, sometimes deadly, sequence of events between members of the same household. This "cycle of violence" is a recurring war of power to keep someone (in most instances, a woman) subservient through physical or emotional abuse and fear. At the slightest provocation, the aggressor ridicules his victim. His frustration and anger quickly escalate to slapping, pushing, beating and, all too often, assault with a deadly weapon.

The complex nature of relationships and dependencies, emotional and economic intimidation, keep battered partners from walking out. Through repeated belittlement and "punishment" for alleged offenses, abusers reinforce their partners' low self-image and feelings of unworthiness. When efforts to placate abusive partners fail to avert another violent episode, battered partners blame themselves.

Caregivers and first-responders can help victims of domestic violence understand that they did not provoke or deserve abusive behavior. The blame is not theirs to

14

shoulder. Chapter IV discusses how to recognize the battering cycle, regardless of which partner is the batterer, and assist battered partners in seeking help.

SEXUAL ASSAULT

Short of murder, rape, historically, has been considered the worst atrocity against a human by a human. Rape represents the most demeaning, denigrating act of dominance of one individual over another. Conquering armies of most every conceivable race raped women and girls as the ultimate, final insult.

Forced sexual intercourse, oral or anal sex are classified as "sexual assault." Research has shown that this crime is seldom the result of an uncontrollable libido, but rather of unbridled rage and a demonstration of power and control.

Nearly 30 percent of women who were sexually assaulted knew their attacker. Whether they were assaulted by strangers or people known to them, victims describe the same feelings of violation, fear, anger, shame and, sometimes, culturally conditioned guilt.

Attitudes toward rape and its victims ebb and flow with the tide of values. Reflecting the wave of change is current legislation that safeguards equitable rights for its victims and burgeoning support groups that empower victims to stand together in strength.

Their combined voices are being taken seriously. Law enforcement and other agencies are re-evaluating interrogation methods that may be demeaning and turn the victim into the accused. Interviews that preserve the victim's dignity also place full responsibility for the attack on the assailant and create an atmosphere of support.

ASSAULT AND ROBBERY

Tension between individuals and groups is often the fuel of violence. In fact, more than half of reported assaults occur among people who are not strangers to each other. For males from families that are physically and emotionally stressed by poverty or ethnic discrimination, the potential for violent confrontations with males of similar background is twice that of females.

Nearly 60 out of 1,000 young adults ages 16 to 24 are likely to be injured or die from such confrontations. Ironically, the risk that these youths will become victims of crime is 20 times greater than that of the elderly, who would appear to be the most vulnerable of all groups.

While it would seem logical that the wealthy are most frequently the targets of assaults and robbery, such isn't the case. Most victims are the poor for whom any loss is a financial hardship.

As if the physical injuries incurred during an attack were not painful enough, assault victims also must contend with emotional injury, which can take many times longer to heal. Robbery victims say they, too, experience a violation of "self." This is understandable as possessions have personal meaning and are associated with every individual's unique identity.

Medical and law enforcement personnel are learning more about this link between the physical and emotional trauma experienced by assault and robbery victims. Chapter VI describes victims' reactions and demonstrates productive interactions that facilitate the body/mind healing process.

LOSING A LOVED ONE TO SUDDEN DEATH

Whenever a friend or family member dies suddenly and unexpectedly, it is always an emotionally taxing event for which survivors are unprepared. Whether the death is natural, accidental, suicide, or homicide, those who remain are confronted with more than the irreplaceable loss of a loved one. They now must face their own mortality.

The complexity and range of emotions experienced by survivors are interwoven with the physical demands of sorting out and fitting into busy schedules the tasks associated with a death. It is a crucial, and stressful, time of decision-making, accompanied by a high level of activity that may leave few moments for experiencing and processing anger and subsequent grief.

Survivors' reactions to the loss of a loved one may also include self-recriminations for being unable to prevent the death. Anger and self-blame are common among the family and friends of those who took their own lives as well as the parents of a child lost to Sudden Infant Death Syndrome. With guidance, however, caregivers can help these survivors lift blame from themselves and focus their energies on positive action and renewal.

In Chapter VII responses that encourage progress are matched to a range of survivor reactions.

DISASTERS

Throughout time, the adaptability and resiliency of the human spirit in the midst of crisis has generated countless acts of heroism. When body and mind are fixed on the goal of survival, of self or others, extraordinary feats can be and are achieved.

Our physical world is fraught with natural and human-generated catastrophes. Nature decides when humankind will be challenged with floods, earthquakes, hurricanes, volcanic eruptions, and sweeping fires. While we trust technology for solutions to many of our problems, it has yet to gain control over such calamitous events. They still catch us off-guard, unprepared for their severity and impact.

War, acts of terrorism, mass transit accidents, explosions, and toxic contaminations are all disasters of our own making, yet no less traumatic for those whose lives are physically and emotionally upturned by them. Characteristically spontaneous and uncontrollable, these technology- and population-driven events chart unknown courses for human experience. For yet unknown disasters, we have no frame of reference for effective response.

As we will see throughout the succeeding chapters, many variables contribute to the range of individual reactions to crisis. The personal trauma of disaster victims is often intensified by the magnitude and collective nature of the event. The emotions and behavior of fellow victims sows an already fertile field.

Recognizing the inherent power of individual and group dynamics during stress, caregivers and first-responders can systematically help restore order and calm, guiding victims through recovery. Chapter VIII broadens our ability to respond to disasters in creative, life-preserving ways.

ELDERLY VICTIMS

Technology is much like the Roman god Janus with two opposite faces. Human ingenuity spawns miraculous achievements that prolong and, we hope, enhance the qualify of life. Invention's other side is darker

Since the dawn of man, the growth and well-being of cultures has been predicated on the model we call "extended family." Those who reached old age lived and died among the young. During the 20th-century, the face of the Western World has aged, and the new model sets the elderly adrift. As their numbers increase, so do abuses against them. As their support systems disintegrate, so do their capacities to protect themselves from crime, neglect, and physical and sexual abuse.

Elderly victims suffer inexcusable hardships. Crimes against them are particularly devastating as their emotional defenses and physical resiliency may have been worn down by economic distress and failing health. Brittle bones are easily shattered and slow to mend. Slow to meliorate, too, is the fear of re-victimization. For the older victim on a limited income, the theft of funds earmarked for food, medicine, or heat can have life-threatening consequences.

It is difficult to conceive that fathers, mothers, grandmothers, and grandfathers can so easily be disregarded and cast off. For this growing segment of the population, individual and community support make the difference between merely living through victimization and restoring the quality of life.

Chapter IX highlights strategies for preventing abuses against the elderly and suggests helpful responses to those who have experienced victimization.

Another segment of the population largely ignored and uniquely vulnerable to abuse and crime are the blind, deaf, and other individuals who are physically and mentally challenged.

CHILDREN AS VICTIMS

Sirens screamed through the intersection. When the ambulance arrived at the emergency room entrance, two nurses and a doctor were waiting for its precious cargo: a two-and-half-year-old girl with broken ribs who had been forced to swallow cocaine. Medics propelled the gurney with its fragile payload through the double doors into the green brightness. Survival now boiled down to seconds.

We want to believe that all babies and young children get the tender loving care they deserve. Tragically, many do not. Child abuse and neglect are the ugly stains on our national conscience that stubbornly resist efforts to wash them away.

A billboard campaign launched in recent years reminded and warned: "Never hurt a child. Never." Children whose only and brief experience of life teaches fear and distrust suffer more than physical pain. Emotional scars may permeate their everyday lives.

Like physical abuse, sexual abuse catapults children into a topsy-turvy world where adults who should be protectors become persecutors. The imposed unnatural sexual relationship places upon these children the added burden of guilt and shame.

Revealing the dark secret, they fear, would mean abandonment, retribution, or even death. So victimized children remain silent until the burden becomes too heavy to bear. Intervention presents unique challenges for caregivers and professionals. Chapter X offers guidelines for identifying victims of child abuse and neglect.

For adults and children, surviving victimization is a walk through fear and pain toward the ultimate goal, reintegration. Getting there takes time, understanding, and a little help from friends.

CHAPTER II

DEALING WITH CRISIS

Family, friends, and professionals may become involved in crisis intervention accidentally or intentionally. In either case, their primary goal is to become a buffer between the victim and the event or person that threatens the victim's physical or emotional well-being. Intervention is an active, though temporary, entry into the life of another to guide that person from crisis to self-determination. As caregivers, we are called upon to do something, NOW.

Victims *react* to crisis. Caregivers can learn to *respond* appropriately.

Crisis can be broken down into three broad categories:

- Interpersonal
- Intrapersonal
- Situational

During an interpersonal crisis, stress escalates between one person and another. The players may be husband and wife, or Group A and Group B.

An intrapersonal crisis results when stress within a person creates inner turmoil, acute depression, or antisocial behavior.

A situational crisis is usually a sudden, external stressor, such as an accident or disaster, for which the victims are unprepared.

The degree of stress experienced as the result of these crises may range from mild to severe. Developing the skills to identify the types and range of stresses enables caregivers and first-responders to assess which actions and responses are most appropriate.

Like life, this book is a work "in progress." While we cannot anticipate or include every instance when intervention is necessary, we have taken broad strokes to paint a clearer picture of human behavior during severe stress and demonstrate how we interact with it and are effected by it.

Although our primary goal is to ensure survival, we believe our moral responsibility does not end there. Rather, we attach to the preservation of life those ideals and values that make life worthwhile, the necessary and sufficient conditions, or opportunities, that challenge us to develop our greatest potential as stronger, healthier adults.

Well-being is an integrative response to body/mind balance and harmony. Before our emotional selves can be fully actuated, however, our physical selves must be assured of security. For some people, peace of mind takes the form of installing deadbolts on doors, avoiding dark alleys, and walking home with a friend instead of alone.

These people are acting on a physical and psychological need to be safe, wisely assimilating and interpreting information about their environment and exercising caution accordingly. Their protective action completed, they can go about the business of life without becoming immobilized by fear.

Securing our homes and avoiding dangerous places do help reduce the risk of victimization. These "if/then" reactions to perceived threat are grounded in personal perceptions of our environment. We gather information and learn about the world through experience and education. Formal or informal, education is a valuable tool for constructing a meaningful life.

However, learning how to protect ourselves cannot guarantee immunity from victimization. We still get in harm's way. We do well to control ourselves and have little or no control over others and nature. When the unexpected occurs, we are liable to become part of the consequence.

It is during this hiatus in control over themselves and their circumstances that victims are most easily influenced by others. Caregivers and first-responders can bring them into a psychological safety net in which they feel free to ask for help and know that help is available without having to ask.

Regardless of its variability, crisis always poses the potential to disrupt normal thinking and living patterns. Because they have few or no functional defenses learned from similar events, victims sometimes become disoriented and immobilized. They may express feelings such as fear, self-pity, anger, and sadness. In addition, victims may feel guilty over their inability to control their situation.

Keeping these reactions in mind, caregivers and first-responders can respond with sensitivity and compassion. The general guidelines that follow are starting points:

- Be calm, gentle, reassuring, confident, and establish a bond of trust.

- Remove the victim from a harmful environment when appropriate.

- Assess the victim's need for immediate medical attention.

- Suspend personal judgments or prejudices that may lay blame or guilt on the victim.

- Permit the victim to express her emotions.

- Listen, be patient and supportive.

- Avoid personalizing the victim's misdirected anger.

- Fulfill requests for assistance as possible.

- Elicit outside help; refer to advocacy agencies when appropriate.

- Facilitate the victim's progress through empowerment.

Be calm, gentle, reassuring, confident, and establish trust. A crisis may not seem like the time for introductions, but, in fact, exchanging names and addressing the victim as Mr. Jones, Mrs., or Ms. Smith shows respect and establishes new bonds of trust that help rebuild the victim's self-concept.

Whether he is 9 or 99, each individual learns from experience the coping skills that enable him to get from one day to the next with minimal anxiety. This cumulative knowledge of self in relationship to the world is dramatically altered during a severe crisis for which there is no frame of reference. Just as a computer's drive searches its memory for stored information, victims subconsciously search for a corresponding situation on which to base a behavioral response. Finding none can be confusing and disorienting. The victim senses he has no control, which magnifies his panic and fear.

Recognizing the victim's need to regain physical and emotional balance, the caregiver can respond compassionately. Speaking calmly in a soothing, confident tone reassures him not necessarily that "everything will be all right," but rather that the present crisis will pass and he will not have to go through the healing process alone.

Because a crisis has the potential to alter a victim's concept of safety, his health, lifestyle, and relationships, it is best not to make promises that his life will be the same as it was. Most likely, it will not be. Instead, caregivers can encourage the victim to rely on his own unique ability to meet new physical and emotional challenges and cope with future stresses.

Remove the victim from a harmful environment when appropriate. Caregivers' and first-responders' first consideration is always to place life before limb. If the situation is exceedingly dangerous and threatens life, the risk involved in moving an injured victim must be weighed. First-responders are advised not to move the injured or suddenly ill person until they assess the consequence of movement, have applied first aid, or are assured the victim's life is in danger at the scene. If danger of further harm has been ruled out, the seriously injured person can be given care in place until emergency medical service (EMS) arrives.

Assess the victim's need for immediate medical attention. An immediate call for help is the safest action. The National Safety Council recommends first-responders assess a victim's condition or extent of injuries based on the following:

- personal observations

- observations of witnesses to the situation

- direct information provided by the victim (or a medical alert tag)

The first-responder's personal observations of the victim provide her with immediate information about wounds, external bleeding, shock, obviously broken bones, and similar injuries.

Witnesses' observations about the event may help the first-responder assess the potential for less-obvious injuries to the victim.

If the victim is not in shock and able to speak, direct questions about her injuries and pain provide valuable information that the first-responder can pass along to the EMS team, especially if there is a risk the victim may lose consciousness. Medical alert tags worn around the wrist or neck provide life-saving information about the wearer's pre-existing medical condition. Some include a 24-hour telephone number to call in case of emergency.

According to the National Emergency Number Association, 75 percent of the population and 25 percent of the geographic area of the United States rely on the 9-1-1 emergency assistance number. Other emergency numbers are usually listed inside the front cover of local telephone directories. Parents should teach their children how to call for help in an emergency and keep direct numbers for their nearest rescue squad, police, ambulance, doctor, and poison control center near a telephone. A small card with these numbers and other life-saving information is invaluable in a wallet and/or vehicle glove compartment.

To assure the most rapid and appropriate aid reaches the victim, the National Safety Council urges first-responders to gather and relay the following information over the phone to a dispatcher:

1. **Victim's location**—The most important information to convey accurately. Have ready complete street number, city, descriptions of buildings, landmarks, and intersections.

2. **Phone number**—Where rescue personnel can call back and reach the first-responder or someone else who can provide additional vital information.

3. **Clear description of the nature of the emergency**—Enables a dispatcher to send appropriate help. Include the number of victims and any special conditions or circumstances that rescuers should know.

4. **Condition of the victim**—Describe in detail observations such as "breathing has stopped,"

"he is unconscious," or "severe bleeding is present."

5. **Assistance already given**—Describe what has already been, or is being, done for the victim, such as, "Someone is administering CPR."

6. **Approval by the dispatcher to hang up**—Stay on the line until the dispatcher indicates he has all the information he needs. Speak slowly, clearly and as calmly as possible.

Caregivers, first-responders, and volunteers untrained in emergency response can offer valuable assistance by:

- Keeping the road, path, or area around the victim open for rescue vehicles (being careful not to remove evidence or obstruct an investigation)

- Alerting traffic (when applicable) that an emergency situation exists ahead

- Dispersing crowds or minimizing disruption directly near the victim

Suspend personal judgments or prejudices that may lay blame or guilt on the victim. While accidents that cause personal injury account for a large percentage of victimizations, others occur as the result of domestic violence, natural and man-made disasters, and crimes such as rape and assault.

The American Medical Association announced that in 1993 alone, at least one-fourth of all emergency room visits by women were the result of beatings they received by their partners or other family members. Fully half of all battered women are pregnant, and studies conclude that the physical violence unleashed on them is a significant cause of natural abortions and birth defects.

27

First-responders need to assess quickly whether or not a victim of domestic assault is still in life-threatening danger, and, if so, how to safely remove her from danger. The direct question, "Are you injured? Tell me where," supplements first-responders' observations and helps determine the need for immediate medical attention. Caregivers should be aware that battered victims often will hide or deny pain and injuries for fear of abandonment or retaliation by their abusers. Those who come in contact with the victim must guard against letting prejudices about domestic violence and its causes override their objectivity.

Today, throughout much of the modern world, rape is understood not as a sexual act or act of passion, but as a degrading, humiliating act of violence. Fortunately, increasing empathy for victims of sexual assault has transmuted judgmental, harsh, and procedural responses to this crime into more victim-oriented responses sensitive to its potentially devastating impact.

Touching may be appropriate and well-received by some victims and, understandably, inappropriate and threatening to others. First-responders will need to make personal decisions based on each victim's reactions to the trauma just experienced.

Posturing is the silent language of all animals. It signals distress, joy, pain, dominance, subservience, and sends a range of vital organism-to-organism messages. Facing the victim, leaning forward, making direct eye contact, and allowing her to speak uninterrupted, assures her not only that someone is listening, but also that she may speak openly without fear of judgment or condemnation.

By avoiding indictments such as, "That was no place to go alone," or "Why didn't you lock the door?" family and friends, as well as medical and law enforcement personnel, correctly shift blame for the crime where it belongs—to the assailant.

To assure the most rapid, effective assistance reaches the victim, the first-responder must convey complete and accurate information to the dispatcher when reporting the crime. Concrete statements about her condition based on direct observations: "She has been crying hysterically for an hour;" "She is vomiting;" or "She looks dazed and won't speak," are more beneficial to medical and law enforcement personnel than descriptive generalities, such as "She is upset."

Information to convey to the dispatcher:

- Concise statement of the problem

- Extenuating circumstances or precautions

- Complete address where the crisis occurred

- Phone number where the reporting party or another informed person can be reached

Information to receive:

- Name, identification number, and precinct of responding officer

- Number of the police report

- Number of the restraining or protection order, if any

Permit the victim to express her emotions. Listen, be patient and supportive. Avoid personalizing the victim's misdirected anger. Sexual assault is an act of brutality in which the victim is forced to relinquish power over her own body to her assailant. Let her regain control immediately by not dominating her time with analysis of the situation. Remember that she is in pain. Even when the physical pain of the transgression has passed, the emotional pain endures. Like most victims of rape, she may reveal that the sacred inner space that defines her being has been desecrated. Rape victims use words such as "helpless," "violated," "naked," "contaminated," to describe the depth of feelings that take time and support to overcome.

The meaning that a victim attaches to any crisis determines how it will impact her life. Few people associated with the victim understand that an attempted crime against her or him can be as devastating as a successful one. How an assault victim reacts is largely determined by experiences that fostered confidence in handling disruptive events, her emotional health, the degree of violence inflicted upon her, and other stressors diluting her ability to cope.

Crises draw the curious. To protect the rape victim from re-victimization, first-responders should discreetly shield her from onlookers and, if possible, provide a comfortable, private place where an investigation can be conducted.

Female and male victims of sexual assault, or any assault that results in injury, may appear outwardly calm, yet hide fear that the frightening event will recur. First-responders and law enforcement personnel can reassure victims they are now safe. Other helpful responses include:

- **Respect.** Show courtesy and respect to help restore the victim's dignity.

- **Patience.** Reduce pressure on the victim by being patient with his frustration, confusion, and anger.

- **Confidence.** Assure the victim that she has the strength to regain control over her life.

- **Involvement.** Explain reporting and investigative procedures, which allows the victim to feel that she is a partner in resolving the case.

- **Empowerment.** Provide the victim with resources or assistance and support.

In some instances, the victim may need help beyond the initial intervention. Crisis assistance can also be obtained by contacting the following local, state, and federal assistance agencies:

- Health-care delivery systems
- Social Service systems
- Judicial systems
- Religious/ministerial communities
- Educational systems

Offering moral and physical support to a victim of violent crime sounds like a simple, charitable thing to do. It is charitable, but far from simple. In fact, it presents a variety of challenges. Even the most intimate relationships are tested by the event's impact. Loved ones who try to ease the victim's burden now must also deal with their own emotions, shaped, oftentimes, by misconceptions about the causes and effects of sexual assault.

Victims themselves may be difficult to live with after the event. Their fear of recurrence may be very real and debilitating. They may also fear loved ones will reject them because they are perceived as contaminated or at fault. Like a Catch 22, the victim who fears rejection most may actually withdraw from family and friends, who then feel estranged, causing a lose-lose cycle to begin. Some partners may sense the intimacy of their relationship to the victim has been compromised or shattered and, despite their best efforts to compensate for such feelings, the victim may be fully aware that the feelings exist.

31

Caregivers who witness such a break-down in traditional support systems can suggest counseling or a support group.

Like fear, denial is a natural reaction to crisis. "This can't be happening to me" reflects victims' pre-crisis perceptions of their personal inviolability. When a child falls and skins her knee, she runs to her mother, trusting mother will dry her tears, bandage her wound, and make her small world feel safe again. But as her world grows, so, too, does her exposure to crises of varying intensity, and she begins to measure the effects of events in terms of their stress on her.

"Why?" or "Why me?" are the most commonly asked questions of caregivers as victims struggle to establish cause-and-effect relationships in crisis events. By identifying the "because," victims neutralize an event's potency and put it in perspective to their lives. Attributing responsibility to someone or some thing for their undeserved physical and emotional pain enables the victim to see predictability in life once more. It is a natural phase in the recovery process.

Whether or not the victim's cause-and-effect beliefs about the crime are unfounded or illogical is less important than that they be supported. Arguing against her constructs and rationalizing or becoming defensive with her is counterproductive. Clearer thinking will come later. Sharply focused blame often manifests itself through strong emotions. Caregivers can acknowledge victims' rage through neutral, yet supportive statements, such as "I hear you;" or "You are really angry." Simultaneously they can discourage self-blaming assessments that sound like "If only I had...."

Supportive, non-judgmental phrases that help restore self-esteem include:

- I'm sorry it happened.

- I'm glad you can talk with me about it now.

- It wasn't your fault.

- Your reaction to this type of situation is normal.

- Things may never be the same, but you can be stronger.

Phrases that are both trite and nonconstructive and should be avoided include:

- It was God's will.
- Life goes on.
- Time heals all wounds.
- Don't cry. It's OK.
- Forgive and forget.

No one wants to acknowledge that they have lost control in a situation. We take it as a blow to our ego. Yet this is a feeling common to victims in crisis. Caregivers can help victims see that maintaining control in some situations is an unrealistic expectation. People caught up in a sudden crisis for which they are unprepared don't always have the option to control what happens to them. Their normal coping mechanisms may fall short of helping them deal with the potential for disorientation. They may be relieved to learn that their reaction is normal.

Those who have been injured or violated in an event may fantasize about "getting even." Fantasies are a legal and socially acceptable way to retaliate against their perpetrator. Usually, fantasies are a harmless way to dissipate anger. Sometimes, however, angry victims strike out against those who are closest to them—friends, family, and caregivers. As long as their anger inflicts no physical harm, it is best to let it roll off. It, too, shall pass.

At the critical moments following a disruptive event, victims need sensitivity and restoration of balance the most. As they are removed from the hostile environment of the crisis scene and returned to familiar, safer surroundings, their sense of normalcy returns, and fear is allayed. Then victims can begin to mobilize energy on their own behalf.

Helping victims to restore order and structure to their lives is an "enabling" process. Victims rebuild trust in others as well as in themselves. The small steps forward that are a chain of successes build confidence in their ability to deal with future crises. There is security in knowledge that "I can."

Fulfill requests for assistance as possible. Beyond the initial intervention, caregivers and first-responders can perform acts that thoughtfully assist the victim in putting his life back in order. "Assisting," "facilitating," "enabling" imply that those who intervene provide the support the victim needs to stand on her own feet and get on with the tasks at hand. They help restore self-reliance and self-determination.

So, what can caregivers do to assist? Why not begin with the now. Does she need transportation home or to another location? If he is to be admitted to the hospital, is there anything he needs from home or the store? Who is going to take care of his pets? Direct questions that require involvement and self-determination assure victims they are in control, but that help is available.

Caregivers will find the following questions lead to additional ways they can assist:

- What would make you more comfortable?

- Whom would you like me to call?

- Where would you like me to drive you?

- Would you feel more safe if someone stayed with you?

- What would you like to eat/drink?

- Where can I locate the dog's leash? The pet food?

- Would you like me to house-sit when you're at the police station/hospital/funeral home?

Elicit outside help; refer to advocacy agencies when appropriate. Each year, the numbers of adults, children, sick, and elderly who become victims of abandonment, neglect, physical or sexual assault increase dramatically. Despite their age and gender differences, many of these victims share a common dilemma: the lack of a support network once provided by the extended family and community. For these growing segments of the population, inadequate financial resources to reconstruct their own lives place the fiscal burden for their medical care, nutrition, shelter, and clothing on local, state, and federal social service organizations and advocacy agencies.

When family members and friends are ill or in pain, we waste no time in suggesting that they see a physician. Yet we often fail to recognize the early warning signs that indicate someone is being victimized.

Like a wound that festers and is slow to heal, the chronically abused individual, debilitated by fear, can make little progress toward personal growth and self-determination. Professional help may not only relieve his needless physical and emotional pain, but may also save his life. With proper support, victims can make progress through the stages of impact, confusion, and ultimate reconciliation with self.

Case histories have provided social workers and law enforcement personnel with valuable analytical information useful in understanding the impact of victimization.

The questions that follow are based on this research and can help caregivers and first-responders assess when a referral is indicated:

- Is the victim at greater physical or psychological risk because of the violent nature of the victimization?

- Was the victim in a life-and-death situation?

- Is the victim suicidal?

- Is the victim elderly?

- Is the victim a child?

- Is the victim presently coping with other serious stressors that weaken his defenses?

- Does the victim have a family or community support system?

- Does the victim have a history of coping with previous problems?

- Is the victim generally in good health?

- Does the victim have a history of substance abuse?

- Has the person been victimized before?

- Is the victim emotionally paralyzed and unable to make progress?

Whatever the factors that enter into the decision to refer, assistance is available from many professional sources. An excellent place to begin is the Victim Assistance Program coordinated by local law enforcement agencies. Local, state, or federal help is also available through the following categories of agencies:

- Crime prevention/self-defense
- Emergency room, ambulance, crisis hot-line
- Housing assistance
- Financial assistance and counseling
- Legal counseling
- Employment counseling
- Alcohol and drug counseling/rehabilitation
- Mental health counseling
- Day care

As we have stated earlier in this book, our goal and the goal of the agencies listed above is to facilitate the victim's progress through empowerment. It is not so much what caregivers do for the victim as when and how they empower the victim to do for herself.

Rape victims who have the support of family and friends more often tend to prosecute their assailants, which, in turn, makes them feel control is being restored to their lives. Prosecuting their assailant is one of many actions that leaves victims better equipped to psychologically transcend their traumatic experience.

Burglary victims who install deadbolts on their doors, assault victims who park their cars in brightly lit, monitored garages, women who take out restraining orders against abusive partners, are all taking actions that help restore autonomy and control over their own lives.

It has been aptly said that people are as powerful as they feel. Providing a victim with the resources to meet the challenges of current stress builds self-confidence and capacity for resilience to future crisis.

SPECIFIC GROUPS OF VICTIMS

Although the dynamics of crisis intervention vary slightly for unique situations and specific groups of victims, there remain basic tenets applicable in all survival situations. These have been the general response guidelines for caregivers and first-responders already discussed. They facilitate victim survival through a process of transformation.

We have learned that survival is a function of the severity of a crisis and the personal resiliency of its victim. All crisis situations test the physical and emotional mettle of victims and those who courageously come to their aid. Among the categories of crises, disasters become samplers for the range of human potential and creative response.

DISASTERS

Natural and man-made disasters, such as earthquakes, floods, tornadoes, hurricanes, tidal waves, volcanic eruptions, sweeping fires, terrorism, warfare, and transportation accidents, are all catastrophes that involve whole families, communities, even regions.

These devastating occurrences that result in loss of life, limb, and property take a sudden and intense toll on human and financial resources. Mobilizing available help during an emergency often falls to natural leaders who, without thought for their own safety and needs, roll up their sleeves to begin at the beginning.

The National Safety Council suggests that first-responders at the scene of an emergency delegate specific tasks to bystanders as well as to those with minor injuries. For example, an assumed leader can designate someone to go for help who will relay detailed observations about the victims to emergency medical services.

The first-responder may designate someone else to keep emergency routes open, and yet another to disperse crowds, or reduce a victim's anxiety by blocking his view of the disaster.

Appropriate crisis intervention at the critical stages of a natural or man-made disaster lets victims feel more at ease and assures them that competent people are restoring order. When the first phases of an emergency have passed and individual or organizational assistance is no longer available or is withdrawn, disaster victims and survivors may feel abandoned. They may also feel overwhelmed, disillusioned, and depressed by the task of reconstructing their physical, emotional, and financial lives. Family, friends, and caregivers alert to the symptoms of this compounded stress can offer support throughout the victims' transition from dependence to independence.

CHILD ABUSE AND NEGLECT

Because they cannot defend or protect themselves, children are a special group of victims who present unique challenges to professional and non-professional caregivers. Tragically, intervention for the child who has been neglected or battered sometimes comes too late.

Each year in America 5,000 children die of injuries inflicted by parents, live-in partners, baby sitters, and family. Young victims who survive abuse have endured inconceivable pain and suffering. Emergency room physicians and nurses yearly see 150,000 children—fully 10 percent of all child medical emergencies—who have been deliberately burned, beaten, scalded, slashed, or forced to ingest a harmful substance. Of those treated, 30,000 are permanently disfigured or scarred.

Child abuse sounds the alarm that a family unit is dysfunctional. Nurturing relationships have broken down. Family and friends who suspect child abuse should waste no time reporting it to law enforcement authorities.

All states now allow for intervention to protect children while providing immunity from liability to those who report the abuse or neglect.

The physically or sexually abused child may benefit from counseling, which can modify inappropriate actions established within his behavior pattern. Consultation with a counselor can also help parents, or the child's primary caregivers, assess the child's anxiety level and feelings of guilt.

SUICIDE

Every day, men and women, young and old, of every ethnic group, consciously make the choice to end their lives. The reasons for attempted and completed suicides are as varied and complex as an individuals' thought processes, experiences, and internal and external stresses. An isolated, or sudden, incident about which the victim feels shame can precipitate suicidal thoughts, as can the need for relief from depression or pain.

Suicide rates for males are highest in the most competitive societies where performance expectations are unrealistic. In the United States, the number of completed suicides is three times greater for men than for women. Although they attempt suicide one-third as often as females, men select more violent means to ensure their death.

Communications studies over the last two generations quantify the impact of media messages on our perceptions, beliefs, and actions. Television tells us, many times per minute, who we are, what we want, where we are going, and how we are going to get there.

Sitcoms reinforce misconceptions about marriage and relationships. We split our sides in laughter over the trials and tribulations of coupling, when, in fact, married people have been shown to be physically and emotionally healthier than their widowed, divorced, or separated friends. Greater levels of contentment enhance each partner's ability to cope with stress, statistically reflected in this group's lowest of all suicide rates. Among all groups, teenagers—whose young lives hint of promise and future—account for the most startling increase in death by suicide.

For many of us, suicide is incomprehensible, therefore, difficult to anticipate and prevent. Because we can only guess what another is feeling, we must be perceptive of signs that indicate intense pain, hopelessness, helplessness, worthlessness, and loneliness.

When his emotional defense mechanisms have shut down, the suicidal individual may already have distanced himself so much from others that he may no longer be able to ask for help. Survival is a natural instinct, even in those most desperate to escape suffering in life. And it is that flicker of desire to live free of pain that makes intervention possible.

When a life is at stake, there is urgency in responding. Nevertheless, and as difficult as it may be, caregivers should be mindful that suicide is a self-destructive behavior with the potential for victims to take others to their death with them.

Family, friends, caregivers, and first-responders should consider anyone who manifests the following behaviors as a high risk for suicide:

- Previous attempts
- Threats of suicide
- Giving away personal belongings
- Putting one's affairs in order
- Changes in behavior, appetite, sleep patterns
- Distancing from friends and family
- Depression
- Alcohol and/or drug abuse

41

SURVIVING

Understanding the facts and myths surrounding suicide may save a life.

MYTH	FACT
Those who talk about it rarely commit suicide	Eight out of ten completed suicides speak of their intentions beforehand
Suicidal individuals are mentally ill	Upset, depressed, not mentally ill
Suicidal individuals really want to die	Most are ambivalent and want help
There is no correlation between alcohol abuse and suicide	Alcoholism is often a contributing factor
Once suicidal, always suicidal	The period of highest risk is usually brief. With help, the impulses can be reversed.
Being direct in asking if a person is suicidal can encourage an attempt	Asking directly can minimize anxiety and act as a deterrent

Caregivers who encounter someone who is engaged in life-threatening behavior should take slow, progressive steps toward the individual and encourage him to move to a place where he feels safe. First-responders need to take time to build a trusting, not adversarial, relationship. At the same time, they must keep in mind that the life of more than one person may be at risk. Sometimes, despite everyone's best efforts, a suicide can't be prevented.

HOMICIDE AND BURGLARY

Survivors who have lost a loved one as a result of homicide are dealt a double blow. Their grief is intermixed with fear, anger, and even the desire to retaliate against the perpetrator.

Compounding these emotions is the survivors' sudden confrontation with their own vulnerability and mortality, which often intensifies their fear of the perpetrator and extends the healing time.

The loss of human life is always the most difficult loss to deal with. Even when life hasn't been threatened, but lifestyle, or memories have, anxiety is aroused. For the victims of burglary, theft, and larceny, more than just the damage or removal of material possessions is at stake. These victims have lost extensions of themselves, continuity with their past, and the sense of home as a safe harbor.

It is natural to be angry when someone invades our privacy and takes away our connections to ourselves and each other. Caregivers and first-responders who understand this and the dynamics of attachment can be supportive of victims who have lost irreplaceable heirlooms, keepsakes, and memorabilia. Theirs is a real loss to grieve.

CHAPTER III

BRICK WALLS OF THE SYSTEM

Until recent years, the rights of victims of crimes and other crises have received little recognition in judicial chambers. Traditionally, the judicial system's emphasis was on identifying the perpetrators of crimes, developing a case for prosecution under the rules of criminal procedure, and obtaining a conviction in a court of law.

Historically, the rights of the accused were accorded greater protection than the rights of those who had been abused or exploited.

Today, the collective voice of advocacy groups is successfully enlightening the judiciary about past inequities and the needs of victims.

Widespread reform is still in the future, but radical, welcome changes are being made. This is especially true in the area of law enforcement and prosecution. Many states have enacted legislation that provides for: funding to compensate victims for such things as loss of property, or damage to property; funeral benefits for the families of those who are killed as a result of a criminal act; assistance with medical expenses resulting from assault or robbery; financial assistance for counseling victims of, or witnesses to, criminal acts.

There are several ways that a crime is brought to the attention of law enforcement authorities. The victim may choose to report the crime. Medical, mental health, or school personnel, who are required to report an incident as a possible crime, may become involved as a result of injuries received by the victim.

SURVIVING

No matter how law enforcement authorities become involved, once a report has been filed, the victim becomes part of the judicial system. This system is comprised of several components. The branch known as law enforcement is the first and most common contact for victims.

When the perpetrator of the crime is unknown, or unidentified, the victim may never have further contact with the system. However, when a perpetrator is identified and subsequently charged with a crime, the second part of the system, prosecution, becomes important. The third component is the sometimes slow, deliberate, due process that we yet cherish—fair trial by an impartial jury or trial judge in a court of law. If the perpetrator of the crime is convicted, the victim may become involved in the final component, the penal, or parole, system.

We believe that basic knowledge of the judicial system empowers victims of crimes, their families, and other professionals to become proactive in seeking justice.

Victims and their supporters should be encouraged to ask important legal, moral, and ethical questions regarding their rights and protections under the law. It helps them understand why certain lines of questioning must be pursued and specific procedures followed. We hope that such knowledge prevents or lessens the physical, emotional, or financial trauma that sometimes result from law enforcement investigations and criminal proceedings during the prosecution of the case.

Armed with information, victims, family, and friends can be prepared to ask pertinent questions throughout the process. In this way, they help ensure involvement in actions that affect them. Each state or prosecuting jurisdiction may subscribe to particular procedures, but they all share commonalities. The summary that follows is typical of judicial systems throughout the United States.

LAW ENFORCEMENT

It is the responsibility of the law enforcement component of the judicial system to be the "finders of fact" in a criminal investigation. To determine the facts of a reported crime, it is necessary that the investigating officer gather *all* available evidence. Evidence is divided into two types: testimonial and non-testimonial.

Testimonial evidence includes statements and interviews with all victims, suspects, and witnesses involved in the incident. Witnesses may include persons who are located by officers while canvassing the area in which the offense occurred. The "neighborhood canvass" is invaluable when the victim cannot provide detailed information or there are no immediate witnesses to the crime.

Initial interviews can be emotionally traumatic for victims of any crime as they relive an experience over which they had no control. For victims who feel that they very nearly lost their lives, talking about the incident may rekindle fear and anguish. It is important that law-enforcement personnel and the people who are the victim's support system understand that it is natural for the victim to experience a range of emotions and feelings about the crime. They should be encouraged to express them openly, without reservation that others will react negatively or prejudiciously toward them.

Non-testimonial evidence is also called physical evidence. This type of evidence is used to reconstruct the incident, corroborate the statements of victims and witnesses, determine if a crime has been committed and who committed it.

Physical evidence is critical in cases where the victim has died, when there are no corroborating witnesses to verify the victim's statements, or when vandalism or theft is involved. To re-create the crime as accurately as possible, law-enforcement personnel trained in forensics and crime-scene analysis rely on such physical evidence as: fingerprints; firearms ballistics; fibers; hairs; blood; other body fluids; photos of the crime scene and injuries; sketches of the crime scene; and dental material and records.

Keeping the victim informed of procedures, tests, and the reasons behind exhaustive questioning helps alleviate or reduce his physical and emotional stress. When law-enforcement personnel fail to extend such a courtesy, a victim or his support group should ask for clarification. There is nothing secret or magical about any police investigation. The victim is an important part of the investigative team.

PROSECUTION

In some cases the prosecutor's office assigns someone to work with the police during the investigation of major crimes, such as homicide. Generally, however, the prosecutor of a case becomes involved following the arrest of a suspect. It is the prosecutor's responsibility to review the case filing from the law enforcement investigation. This review ensures that all statutory elements of the alleged crime are present, and that the correct crime has been charged. The prosecutor establishes that probable cause exists, in other words, that there is sufficient cause to believe that the suspect arrested was the perpetrator of the crime.

Following the review of the case and its acceptance for filing with the court, the prosecutor becomes responsible for all discussions with the defense attorney concerning possible plea bargaining. She prepares the case for pertinent court hearings, which may include a rights advisement, preliminary hearing, arraignment, legal motions hearing, trial, pre-sentence preparation, and sentencing. A crime victim may be called upon to testify at the preliminary hearing, motions hearing, trial, and sentencing. The need to testify at these levels depends on the nature of the case and whether or not the victim's testimony is critical at that particular level.

The prosecutor maintains open communication with the victim during the repetitive court process. If the prosecutor fails to communicate with the victim or his support system, they should take the initiative and ask questions. As an essential part of the prosecution team, the victim must be informed to be adequately prepared for court hearings by the prosecutor or the person she designates.

COURT

Generally, the court is composed of one judge and his staff, usually a clerk, reporter, and bailiff. As the criminal process continues, one judge may preside over the preliminary hearing and another over the motions hearing and trial. Whether or not this happens depends on the criminal procedure applicable in the state where the proceedings take place.

The responsibility of the judge in any hearing is to ensure that the process follows the rules of criminal procedure applicable to that court. The judge is also responsible for protecting the constitutional rights of the defendant in the case.

The witnesses in most felony cases—any crime punishable by imprisonment—are usually sequestered from the court proceedings during the hearings. This separation maintains the integrity of their testimony and prevents their testimony from being influenced by the testimony of others.

Sequestering witnesses is one of the most difficult aspects of the process for many victims to accept. Victims often say that if the defendant has the right to hear all that is being presented, so, too, should they. From an emotional standpoint, this is easy to understand because the victim has a personal investment in the outcome of the case. Defense attorneys use the argument that the victim's testimony was influenced by what he heard. Victims should be reminded that it is imperative to protect the integrity of the entire proceeding in order to prevent the loss of a conviction on a legal technicality.

Following are suggestions for victims and their support groups when testifying:

- Do not try to memorize what you are going to say before you go into court. Prepare with the prosecuting staff; try to picture the scene and review any documents or records pertinent to your testimony so that you can recall them more accurately when you are questioned.

- Listen carefully to each question. Before you answer, make sure you understand what is being asked. If you do not understand the question, ask for it to be repeated or clarified.

- Take your time. Formulate your answer before giving it.

- Speak clearly so that you will be heard. The court reporter must be able to hear and record your answers.

- Testify as accurately as possible about what you know.

- Answer only the question that is asked. Do not volunteer information not asked for.

- Do not give your personal opinion unless specifically asked to do so. Give only the facts as you know them.

- Remain calm, cooperative, and under control.

Once all the testimony has been presented, the victim should ask to be present in the courtroom during the closing arguments and instructions to the jury. This will allow the victim to observe the jury and develop a sense of the direction the jury may take. The victim should be as prepared as possible for an acquittal as well as for a conviction.

PAROLE

Once a defendant has been found guilty of a crime and sentenced, the incarceration usually occurs in the prison system of that particular state. No matter where the imprisonment occurs, most sentences allow for the possibility of parole within a designated period of time.

The victim or victims may wish to ask the prosecutor when the defendant would become eligible for parole. As that time draws near, the victim may choose to contact the state parole board and request the opportunity to testify at the parole hearing, or provide a letter about the effect that the crime has had on him. It is acceptable for the victim to be very direct in expressing concerns about the release of the defendant. A well-informed parole board can make more appropriate decisions.

With this general discussion of the legal system, we have attempted to empower the victim, his family, friends, and support group, and help prevent re-victimization. The victim who remains an involved, informed member of the team has the greatest assurance that his rights will be protected.

CHAPTER IV

DOMESTIC VIOLENCE

Each of us is unique. We arrive on this earth preprogrammed with a host of idiosyncrasies. Over time, we develop even more habits, tastes, and expectations that define us and make us think, feel, and act differently from the person next door.

When we merge sometimes disparate personalities — through marriage or whatever circumstance brings us together under the same roof — we test our mettle. In good relationships as well as poor ones, there is stress. Relating to each other in peace and harmony requires enormous effort and energy. When any relationship is stressed beyond the coping strategies of its individual members, the results can be explosive.

Any threatened, attempted, or actual physical contact between two or more people within the same household that causes bodily injury, death, or damage to property constitutes domestic violence.

With the coining of the term "nuclear family," a phenomenon of great social and psychological import was identified and labeled. It was just a few decades ago that the miles separating family members in Kennebunk and Carmel began to be measured by the cost of a long-distance telephone call, or the air time from Shreveport to Saginaw.

In the '90s, grandchildren often get to nestle in the nurturing warmth of grandparents' laps only on holidays. Parents many times must rely on neighbors for advice on relationships and child-rearing. Or on no one. The typical family of four is no longer typical.

Without the support of parents, friends, and community, many families accrue stress until they reach a critical emergency state. Lacking effective coping skills, individuals may feel their problems are without solutions. When one or more members are out of control, someone is liable to be seriously injured or killed.

While anyone in a household can be a target of domestic violence, women are most often its victims. According to the American Medical Association, domestic violence is the leading cause of injury to American women age 15 to 44. Each year, more than two million women are battered by husbands or lovers. Thirty-five percent of female emergency room visits are for injuries sustained during battering. The FBI reports that half of all women murdered in the United States are killed by boyfriends or husbands who have lost control.

It is not uncommon for men to be victims of domestic violence, and whenever injury to both male and female occur during an incident, caregivers and first-responders should not assume that the male is the abusive partner. Males are simply less likely to report cases of abuse than females.

Unfortunately, only 5 percent of domestic violence cases are discovered during medical interviews. Physicians may not recognize the physical and emotional signs of longtime trauma, or they may be reluctant to broach the question of abuse with their patient for fear they will offend if she or he isn't being abused.

This chapter describes the characteristics of battered women and the men who batter. Understanding the Cycle of Violence—how it begins, escalates, and destroys a relationship—will enable family members and law enforcement personnel who intervene in domestic violence to offer more effective assistance.

Rhonda and Phil lived together for almost a year before they married. Rhonda had witnessed Phil's temper, but she had never imagined that he was capable of hurting her.

Less than a month after their marriage, Phil came home from work one evening in a bad mood. When Rhonda asked him what was wrong, he yelled at her to mind her own business and stop controlling him. For emphasis, he pushed her into the corner. The more she resisted, the more violent he became. Before Phil had unleashed all his frustration on Rhonda, she had a black eye and her ribs were badly bruised where he had kicked her repeatedly.

As the months went by, the beatings became more frequent and more severe. When her friends asked her why she was always bruised, Rhonda said she was clumsy and fell often. The young wife didn't understand her husband's anger at her, but she recognized when he was losing control. She was worthless, he told her time and again. Yet, after each beating, Phil would say he loved her and showered her with affection, as he had early in their relationship. Rhonda learned how to push him to get it over with. She needed to hear him say he really did love her. Their cycle of violence had become predictable.

BATTERING CYCLE

The dynamics of domestic violence, often referred to as the Cycle of Violence, or the Battering Cycle, was first identified by Lenore Walker, EdD. Walker's studies demonstrated that battered women are neither constantly abused, nor is their abuse inflicted at totally random times. Over time, the cycle of abuse becomes more frequent and severe. Understanding the cyclical nature of battering and the emotional cycles of the batterer is critical to prevent such incidents and help victims and potential victims recognize their onset.

The Battering Cycle involves three stages:

- Tension-building stage
- Acute battering incident
- Honeymoon stage

Relationship dynamics occur during each stage.

Tension-Building Stage

The tension-building stage often escalates over a long period of time. As the frequency of cycles increases, the duration of this stage decreases. During the tension-building stage, the abuser is frustrated and becomes increasingly irritable and coercive. In classic cases, the woman is intent on keeping the peace. Early in the cycles, she tries to avert a recurrence by anticipating and fulfilling her partner's desires and whims. She may also try to avoid him altogether in hopes that the opportunity for him to abuse her will pass. But it does not. He becomes verbally abusive and may slap her. As he loses control, so does she. The tension builds rapidly.

During this stage the woman is often ashamed or embarrassed that their relationship and her household are out of control and conceals her partner's behavior from friends and family. For a time, she continues to function in her job environment and accepts the responsibility for many of the problems. She denies the reality of the violence, her anger at being a victim, and even the fear that motivates her actions.

Acute Battering Incident

This stage can last between 2 and 24 hours. The tension between the couple becomes unbearable and is uncontrollably discharged. The precipitating factor is usually some outside event, unrelated to the woman's behavior and, thus, is unpredictable. The violence is most severe during this stage. It is a pivotal point when most initial contacts are made with police, medical personnel, and advocates. If the police are called, the woman often protects her batterer and does not press charges. She feels that escape is impossible and becomes passive, "waiting out the storm."

The Honeymoon Stage

To assuage his overwhelming guilt and remorse, the batterer is affectionate and loving, presents gifts, and promises that he will never hurt her again. He is terrified of abandonment. Using guilt, he convinces her how selfish it would be to "break up the family" and leave him when he needs her most. His own guilt tells him his behavior is wrong, but he is afraid to seek help. Out of her own fear of abandonment and, perhaps, her continuing love for him, she desperately wants to believe that he will change and she clings to that hope. The two re-bond in warmth and intimacy.

RECURRENCE

But the hiatus is temporary. The Battering Cycle continues. In each recurrence, the tension building and honeymoon stages become shorter and shorter. Eventually, the cycle becomes so accelerated that intervention is unavoidable. The woman is often injured to the extent that she needs emergency medical attention, or the physical and emotional strain become so unbearable that she seeks help.

TACTICS

Incidents of domestic violence are almost always battles over power and control. Abuse is an aggressive, outward assertion of control over another. This section describes the methods used to establish power.

Physical Abuse

Physical abuse consists of activities such as grabbing, pushing, shoving, hitting, slapping, choking, pulling hair, punching, and kicking. As it escalates, it becomes more aggressive, more violent, more demeaning. Finally, the abuser resorts to throwing potentially lethal objects at the victim, beating, or assaulting the victim with a weapon.

Isolation

The abuser also exerts power over her by controlling what she does, when she does it, whom she sees and talks to, and where she goes. In effect, she becomes his prisoner.

Emotional Abuse

Psychological games are another way the abuser effectively establishes and maintains control over his victim. Consciously and subconsciously, he debases and shames her, and she begins to place greater value in his assessment of her than of her own. She believes the labels he has given her; she is worthless, dependent, incompetent, crazy. Eventually, she becomes a victim of her low self-esteem.

Economic Abuse

The abuser also exercises financial control. Often, he will reduce the risk of her abandonment by restricting her potential to become financially independent. He may prevent her from getting or keeping a job, or insist on control of the income she earns. To reinforce his power over her and ensure her dependency on him, he doles out meager allowances and insists that she ask him for money, even for essentials.

Sexual Abuse

Sexual abuse occurs whenever the woman is forced to engage in sexual acts against her will. When the abuser's fantasy of power extends to controlling the sexual parts of his partner's body, he regards her as little more than a possession, a sexual object at his disposal. To intensify his sense of power, he may rape her or sadistically assault her sexual organs.

Using Children

Tragically, children are usually caught in the middle of power struggles between parents or between a single parent and his or her partner. Children in a dysfunctional household become both weapon and target. The abuser uses them to inflict guilt on their mother, sometimes holding them up as testimony of her short-comings. The complaints he hurls against them affirm her worthlessness and keep her self-esteem in check. She is inadequate both as a lover and a mother. He makes derogatory remarks about her to the children, uses them to convey disparaging messages, or manipulates visits with them to harass her.

Threats

Abusers exercise emotional, physical, and financial control through action and threat of action. Threats may range from additional injury, withdrawing financial support, taking the children, to committing suicide. Whatever the threat, it illicits the desired conditioned response from her, and she remains under her abuser's control.

Male Privilege and Intimidation

The man who abuses a woman has little regard for her. She is chattel, a sexual object, a servant to be dispatched at whim. He believes himself the "master of his castle," and, unwittingly, the abused woman perpetuates his self-concept. Coined "male privilege," this attitude worsens with time and spawns increased assertiveness. He manifests his superiority and dominance through posture, gestures, menacing looks, and a loud voice. Or he may intimidate her by destroying objects of personal value to her.

WHY WOMEN CAN'T LEAVE

In order to assist more victims devastated by family dysfunction, psychologists and counselors have found it necessary to identify the varied and complex reasons why abused women stay in violent relationships. A combination of factors, summarized briefly here, are usually sufficient to make a woman feel she can't leave.

- **Frequency and severity.** The battering may occur over a relatively short period of time. During the honeymoon stage, the abuser may tell the woman, and she may be convinced, that each battering was the last. Generally, the less severe and frequent the incidents, the more likely that she'll stay.

- **Her childhood.** The woman reared in a home where her mother was beaten for minor infractions may accept abusive behavior as a natural way in which men "punish" women who can't meet their expectations and demands. She is also likely to stay if she learned from her parents that it is acceptable to hit someone who has done something wrong. She, or one of her siblings, may have been the victim of child abuse or incest.

- **Economic dependence.** The woman with few or no marketable skills has difficulty visualizing any real alternative to her and her children's economic dependency on the batterer. To avoid the unknown, she exchanges abuse for security. She may not be aware of—or may be reluctant to seek—outside assistance. She may reject the idea of "going on welfare." If her partner controls their finances, she may have no access to cash, checks, or important documents needed to begin life on her own.

- **Fear.** An abusive partner envisions himself omnipotent in his home. A battered woman will find it difficult to protect herself from such assumed and imagined power. Her fears of him are justified. He may threaten to take revenge if she reports him to the police. She may protect him by denying the abuse, afraid that disclosure might cost him his job and remove the sole source of family income. She may fear the condemnation and wrath of both families if she leaves or reports his abuse to authorities.

- **Isolation.** Friends and family made uncomfortable by ugly scenes and tension may inadvertently withdraw the very support the abused woman needs most. After he has systematically destroyed her other relationships, the abuser becomes her only psychological support system. If she is unaware of community services to assist her and her children, she may feel isolated and trapped. In years past, few professionals were trained in the complexities of battering, and medical personnel, who could also refer the victim to assistance programs, often did not identify battering incidents until severe injury or death had resulted.

  Often, the abuser threatens to kill her, the children, and anyone else she involves if she reports him, thus cutting off communications with potential helpers. Relatives and friends who occasionally offered shelter may be unwilling to extend themselves when she needs them most. Sometimes, the last one to recognize the domestic violence is the battered woman. She may sense that her home is dysfunctional, yet be unaware that no one has the right to beat her.

- **Low self-esteem.** Learned helplessness is a pattern of behavior reinforced by the perception that one's actions are consistently ineffective. A battered woman believes that nothing she does will change her situation. She is convinced that she is incapable of functioning on her own. Depression sets in and the learned helplessness becomes self-perpetuating. It gets in the way of self-preservation, acting on her own behalf, and being her own advocate.

  When she discovers that her partner is only violent with her, she presumes something is wrong with her. She accepts his explanation that she "deserved" the punishment he meted out, and that if she would only improve or stop making mistakes, the punishment would stop.

Finally, myths and misconceptions about domestic violence contribute to the social stigma attached to its victims. The victim is embarrassed and ashamed to admit to her situation because of the prejudices she anticipates.

- **Beliefs about marriage.** Cultural or religious expectations about the role of wife as the obedient and dutiful servant to her husband place great pressure on a battered woman to accept her fate. She may fear social or religious ostracism or condemnation if she puts self-preservation ahead of her marriage vows. Further, she may have grown up with no role models for relationships free of violence.

- **Beliefs about her partner.** The emotionally dependent woman simultaneously loves and fears her partner. She may pity him, making excuses for his behavior by blaming his boss, his mother, anyone but him. Additionally, she may believe that she is the only one who can help him overcome his problem. The abused woman may also believe that if she were to leave, her partner would track her down.

SAFETY PLAN FOR VICTIMS

- Get rid of weapons in the house, especially if someone in the household has a history of becoming violent.

- Request neighbors be alert to strange or threatening noises and call police if they become alarmed.

- Always keep some money hidden.

- Have extra keys for the car and house in a safe place.

- Have important documents and other valuable items readily accessible, such as:

  - Bank accounts
  - Insurance policies
  - Marriage license
  - Driver's license
  - Valuable jewelry
  - Social security numbers (of all family members)
  - Birth certificates (including the children's)

- Keep a small bag ready with extra clothing. Have the items hidden in one central, accessible place—garage, closet, or exercise bag in the trunk of the car—where they will not be cut off from immediate access during a violent episode.

- Above all, don't hesitate to call the police!

Law enforcement personnel frequently encounter domestic violence situations in which they instinctively know the woman is in severe danger of injury or death. The risk factor, or lethality, checklist that follows can assist family, friends, and professionals in assessing the degree of danger to individuals in the household.

While not all factors need to be present for the threat to be severe, intervention is justified when the abuser demonstrates any of the following behaviors:

RISK FACTOR CHECKLIST

- Calls the victim demeaning, derogatory names
- Blames the victim for her/his personal injury
- Is unwilling to turn the victim loose
- Is obsessed with the victim
- Is hostile toward interventionists
- Is raging
- Appears to be out of control
- Appears to be in a volatile or dysfunctional relationship
- Makes threats to injure or kill the victim
- Has history of previous incidents of extreme violence
- Has history of attempted suicide
- Has access to the victim
- Has access to guns and other weapons
- Uses or abuses alcohol or other controlled substances
- Thinks of him/herself as having the right to "correct" or "punish" the victim
- Envisions him/herself committing violent acts

STALKING

The last warm glow of sunset spread across the deck. Amanda and her boyfriend sipped wine and laughed, delighting in the newness of their relationship. She was relieved by its lightness. He was so unlike the possessive, jealous man she had broken up with weeks before. She was comfortable with this new intimacy and her companion's easy manner. The doorbell was an intrusion neither of them wanted.

Moments later, a puzzled, frightened Amanda returned to the deck. Inside the small gift-wrapped box that had been left outside her apartment door were two silver

bullets, each with a tag: "This one is for you, Amanda.
This one is for your boyfriend."
She knew the writing all too well. Her face went white.

It can happen to anyone. Any time of the day.
Anywhere. You feel uncomfortable. Uneasy. You sense
you are being followed. Someone is stalking you. In fact,
200,000 people in this country are stalking somebody
every year.

Only 17 percent of those stalked are highly
recognized celebrities. More than twice that many are
ordinary citizens preyed on, not by a stranger, but by
someone they know. The stalker's motives may vary from
fantasy fulfillment and gaining, maintaining, or
controlling a relationship, to causing injury or even death.

Stalking is a word we associate with a stealthy predator
and an unsuspecting prey. Unfortunately, that prey can be
your best friend, your daughter, or even you. Anyone
who follows you, or clandestinely observes your behavior
with malicious intent, is a stalker and may be dangerous.

A perpetrator crosses the fine line between harassment
and stalking when he intimidates his victim into fearing
for her safety.

Fear can be a stimulus to action. Yet stalking victims
too often brush off initial incidents, hoping that they are
isolated and will not recur. Victims may fail to report
stalking for fear of being labeled paranoid when they say
that someone is following them.

As this repetitive, threatening conduct gains wider
recognition, more and more states are placing anti-
stalking laws on their books. These laws provide for stiffer
and stiffer penalties with each offense. Many states with
such laws have experienced a tragedy that was the impetus
for protective legislation.

If local police departments are to put teeth into those
laws, offenses must be brought to their attention. Family
and friends should insist that stalking victims report all

incidents to law enforcement authorities, either by phone or in person at the police department.

Before others can help, they need to know that you are in a threatening situation. Tell family members, friends, even your employer, that you are being stalked. They should be aware of the risk to you, and their observations may provide valuable testimony if needed. When the incident recurs, be ready with an auto-focus camera and quickly snap mug-shots of the stalker. The act of doing this may be enough to scare him off, and you have evidence for the police.

If you are being followed while in your car, drive to the nearest police station and give the reporting officer the license number and description of the stalker's car. If you are nowhere near a police station, drive to a very public place where you can get access to a telephone. Remember, the stalker is exercising mind control over you. Your greatest protection is rationality.

You can take precautions to help reduce your risk of being stalked. If you believe that you are being stalked, take action immediately.

- Change routines. Vary the time and direction that you leave home, walk, or drive to lunch, the bank or the store.

- Let your employer know that you need to be escorted to your car after work.

- Keep detailed records of the dates, times, and locations that you have been stalked. Record any observations about the stalker and his behavior that may be useful to police.

- Take out a restraining order against the stalker if he has been identified. The order makes subsequent contact with you an offense.

- Maintain a close, working relationship with authorities to enable them to apprehend and convict the stalker who does not obey a restraining order.

CHAPTER V

SEXUAL ASSAULT

Every 360 seconds, a woman is raped. If that sounds unbelievable, consider that one in four women will be sexually assaulted in her lifetime.

Rape is a personal crime of violence. It is not a sexual act, but a power play. During the assault, the rapist discharges rage, anger, or frustration through the sexual act. As the assailant gains control over his victim's body, his victim's feeling of powerlessness increases

Although rape violates the whole person and severe injuries can result, the greatest damage is to the inner *self*. While victims usually seek treatment for their physical injuries, they rarely talk about this inner violation. Yet, the long-term ramifications to the ego, belief systems, and inner space make recovery more complicated than from flesh wounds alone. The rapist penetrates the most private part of his victim—her psyche.

"Contamination." "Shame." "Guilt." The feelings associated with this personal crime are shaped by our upbringing, by society and by our own personal crises.

This chapter focuses on victims' reactions to sexual assault and steps that first-responders and caregivers can take to ease the pain and trauma and promote healing.

SURVIVING

RAPE

Shawna nearly burst out of the mall into the sunny warmth of a Saturday afternoon. Her shift at the department store was over, and all she could think about was the evening ahead. She and friends were going to the amusement park. She hardly noticed the short man leaning on the car next to hers, until he turned suddenly and pulled a knife.

"Unlock it and get in," he ordered her, pushing her into the passenger seat, then sliding behind the wheel. Shawna was terrified. He drove through the suburbs, then down a dead-end road. All the while he kept a knife to her side, he talked as though they were on a date.

He pulled into a secluded parking lot. "Get in the back seat and take off all your clothes," he ordered. She shivered. Her mind raced. How could she get away? He told her what he wanted, but she sat frozen. Shawna had no experience with oral sex, in fact, she was still a virgin. She hoped oral sex was all he wanted. But it wasn't. Shawna was so tense with fear and pain, she hurt all the way to her shoulders.

Somehow, she allowed her mind to let go of what he was doing to her so she could concentrate on his appearance, the clothes he wore, anything about him she could tell the police. When he finally got off her, he rolled her on her stomach. With a sweep of his arm, he wound her pantyhose around her neck. "Die, you bitch, die!" he said, stretching out each word as he pulled the hose tighter and tighter. She choked and gasped, struggled and twisted to loosen his hold. But she wouldn't die.

Suddenly, he yanked the pantyhose from her neck and used them to tie her hands behind her back. In an instant, he was behind the wheel. The tires squealed as he raced from the deserted lot. Shawna was sure he was taking her to the mountains to kill her and dump her body. About fifteen minutes later he slammed on the brakes and quickly gagged her.

70

For some reason, he kept opening and closing the door, so she was never sure if he was still there. After what seemed like eternity, she raised herself until she could reach behind her for the door handle. When the door swung open, she took a deep breath and nearly fainted. She was in a park.

Two young men jogging past untied her and called the police. Shawna was alive. That was all she could think about. She had planned an evening with friends. Instead, she spent the evening at a hospital where doctors and nurses prodded, poked, and collected samples of her assailant's semen, hair and saliva. She felt cold. Very cold.

While her friends partied, Shawna spent the summer in fear and isolation. Her family tried not to act like it was all her fault, but sometimes Shawna sensed they believed she could have prevented it. The nightmare continued when the pregnancy test came back positive. Shawna and her parents struggled through the question of abortion.

During the rape, life seemed so precious. Now, thoughts of ending hers permeated everything. She hardly recognized her reflection in the mirror, that girl with the long scar around her throat. It was the other scars, on her heart and soul, that would take time to heal. A long time.

Six months after the rape, the police caught her assailant. Her complete and accurate description rendered a police composite drawing that was a perfect likeness. From somewhere deep within she mustered the strength to confront him in the courtroom, not once, but three times. She hadn't been his only victim. The judge took that into consideration when he sentenced her assailant to life imprisonment, without parole.

Her rape occurred 12 years ago. But the nightmares are still with her, and she won't go to the mall alone. A faint, pink line is still visible across her neck. But it's the invisible scars that color her relationships and her future.

Victims of rape should always seek immediate medical attention. The medical examination serves two purposes. First, the victim is treated for injuries and tested for sexually transmitted diseases. Second, the medical report provides important information for the investigation.

Rape victims may develop physical reactions to stress, such as insomnia, nausea, a change in eating habits, listlessness, and fatigue. Most, like Shawna, are emotionally traumatized as well. Left unchecked and unresolved, intense emotional reactions may lead to depression and anxiety disorders that require professional counseling.

Every victim of rape is unique in the way she perceives and internalizes her trauma. Understanding victims' most common reactions enables first-responders, professionals, family, and friends to offer appropriate, helpful responses.

REACTION   Victims are often upset and need calming.

RESPONSE   Be patient and allow the physical processes involved in the crisis to run a natural course. Don't make demands for immediate self-control. Help the victim regain control in a reasonable time frame.

REACTION   Victims sometimes hide their fear and anxiety behind a mask of restrained control.

RESPONSE   Avoid assuming that the external calm actually reflects how the victim feels. Give her either direct or unspoken permission to express her fears, frustrations, anger.

REACTION   Victims may continue to experience fear after medical personnel or police arrive.

RESPONSE   Professionals must directly reassure the victim that she is safe. Reassure her, too, that continued assistance will be available from medical and law enforcement resources who do care about her total well-being.

REACTION   Victims frequently expect to be blamed for what has happened. They will often blame themselves.

RESPONSE   Place all blame on the assailant. Continually reassure the victim that you, and others, do not blame her. Avoid making comments that might be interpreted as blaming the victim. For example, "You probably shouldn't have worn that dress."

REACTION   Victims may perceive that police or medical personnel are in a hurry and consequently become more pressured and confused.

RESPONSE   Communicate patience and a willingness to spend the time necessary to help understand that police and medical personnel are trying to obtain as much information as quickly as possible to facilitate an arrest.

REACTION   Victims need help to regain a feeling of control over their lives.

RESPONSE   Clearly explain all investigative procedures and allow the victim to feel that she is a partner in resolving the case. (Later in this chapter, we list questions that professionals will ask to aid in apprehending the perpetrator.) Avoid putting the victim in a passive role. Loved ones should encourage the victim to be responsible for family decisions and duties.

REACTION   Victims feel their assault is very important and seek sympathy and understanding.

RESPONSE   Express understanding of the importance that the victim places on the assault. Professionals should not treat anyone as a "routine case."

REACTION   Victims often experience humiliation, shame, or a loss of dignity.

RESPONSE   Be courteous and respectful of the victim. Help restore her feeling of self-worth by treating her with dignity.

REACTION   Victims often accuse the police or others of not protecting them. She may express anger at the officer who is investigating the assault, or a father who was not available to give her a ride home from work.

RESPONSE   Acknowledge the victim's right to be angry, but help her redirect her anger toward the assailant. Avoid becoming defensive or argumentative, especially with an accusing victim.

REACTION   Victims usually fear a recurrence of the assault.

RESPONSE When the victim is calm and able to listen attentively, help her plan for the future. Professionals should give the victim information about how to be more safe in many kinds of environments.

DATE/ACQUAINTANCE RAPE

Inviting your lab partner over to your apartment for spaghetti after the study group breaks up seems like a friendly thing to do. After all, he's worked next to you twice a week for nearly four months. But are you really safe? Maybe. Only maybe.

One out of six women in college will be raped by someone she knows. *Newsweek* reported that a study conducted by the National Center for the Prevention and Control of Rape found that 92 percent of adolescent rape victims were acquainted with their attackers.

Familiarity with the victim's attacker gave this type of sexual assault its name: "acquaintance" or "date" rape. It is the most controversial and misunderstood form of sexual assault, surrounded by misconceptions and untruths.

Ignorance about date rape has met headlong with increasing media attention, fueling the controversy. In blaming the rape victim for being in the wrong place at the wrong time or leading on her assailant we are overlooking the most important aspect of date rape. At any time, any place, at any stage of intimacy, the woman has the right to say "no" and have her wish respected.

If her date continues to make unwanted sexual advances, the situation suddenly changes. Sex forced on an unwilling victim, through threats, tone of voice, physical endangerment, weapons, or sheer difference in physical size between the attacker and his victim is rape. Rape by a friend or acquaintance is as much a violation of a woman's body as rape by a stranger.

MYTHS ABOUT DATE/ACQUAINTANCE RAPE

MYTH   Rape is always committed by a crazed stranger.

REALITY   Most women are raped by "normal" acquaintances. In fact, more than 60 percent of rape victims know their assailant.

MYTH   If a woman lets a man buy her dinner, she owes him sex.

REALITY   No one owes sex as payment to anyone else, no matter how expensive the dinner.

MYTH   Agreeing to kiss or pet with the man means that she has agreed to intercourse.

REALITY   Everyone has the right to say "no" to sexual activity at any time, regardless of what has precededit.

MYTH   Women lie about being raped, especially when they accuse someone they know.

REALITY   Rape really happens, to people you know, people like you; by people you know, and people like you.

Where does seduction leave off and rape begin? Men and women may have different perceptions about what takes place during intimate moments. Seduction and/or flirtatiousness may lead to intimacy that escalates beyond casual, acceptable contact to foreplay. When the woman retreats to safer territory, she expects the man to comply with her boundaries.

A useful distinction to keep in mind is that seduction involves no force and occurs when a woman, as a result of erotic play or some other enticement, agrees to have sex. Acquaintance or date rape occurs when seduction fails, and the man forces sex with the woman despite her protests and without her agreement.

The pretty blond from his literature class obviously had downed quite a few beers. Haley had been at the frat party for about an hour, and he'd been watching her put them away. She spoke idly with one of his frat brothers, and he interrupted her slow, slurred speech to hand her another foaming draft.

"You look great," he told her. And she did. When he cocked his head toward the room, his buddy took the hint and ambled off. Haley talked for a few minutes, getting close enough to stroke her hair, then her shoulder, carelessly, casually letting his hand cup over her breast, down her sleek abdomen and across her hard buttocks. She smiled, and took another sip, then leaned toward him. His tongue found her mouth warm and wanting.

Haley offered his open hand, inviting her to the bedrooms upstairs. She hesitated, then placed her hand in his.

As he stretched his full weight on top of her, she closed her eyes. She felt so light-headed and his deep kisses made her want to forget where she was. Haley slid his fingers from between her legs to unzip his fly.

"Don't," she pleaded, twice, then a third time. "I can't. I don't want to go all the way."

He held her tiny wrists above her head. His free hand tugged at her panties. She struggled to slide out from under him, but his weight kept her in place. His knee pried her legs apart and he thrust into her with such force that she needed to catch her breath. In less than a minute, he ejaculated.

SURVIVING

"I want to see you again," Haley told her, already planning sex with her in his room when his roommate was gone.

For weeks, she felt guilty, dirty, and frightened. Anyone who had seen her head for the bedroom with Haley would never believe she had been raped. She had too much to drink and she made the mistake of going upstairs with him. But she hadn't asked to be raped. She never confronted Haley or reported the rape. He never thought that he committed a crime.

EFFECTS OF DATE/ACQUAINTANCE RAPE

The story of the pretty coed is real. Sadly, it is repeated again and again on campuses and in communities across the country. The coed's reactions are familiar to rape counselors and therapists. Most rape victims experience "rape trauma syndrome," a term coined in the early '70s as a result of research by Drs. Ann Burgess and Lynda Holmstrum. The syndrome outlines definable stages of trauma:

- **Fear of being alone.** This may be especially acute shortly after the rape and may continue.

- **Fear of men.** Victims of acquaintance/date rape are left doubting their choice of men, wondering if they will ever again date safely. Victims wonder if they will be able to trust their own judgment and others again.

- **Sexual problems.** Because the sex act is now associated with violence, victims have difficulty regaining normal, satisfying sexual relations.

- **Depression.** Depression may come and go over an extended period of time.

78

- **Fear of retaliation.** This may be a very legitimate fear, especially when criminal charges are being filed.

- **Afraid to trust.** Learning to trust again takes time, and courage.

- **Physical symptoms of stress.** Insomnia, headaches, eating disorders, and others may last for months or several years.

- **Strong feelings.** These usually include helplessness, anger, guilt, embarrassment, shame, and anxiety.

- **Denial.** Depending on the individual, the victim may not want to talk about the rape, but rather repress it, saying she just wants to forget it ever happened.

- **Resolution.** This is the constructive stage during which the victim deals with fears and feelings and begins to regain a sense of control over her life.

WHAT FAMILY AND FRIENDS CAN DO

When friends and loved ones respond to a victim of rape with emotional support and caring, they help her cope with the immediate crisis and make progress toward long-term recovery.

Counseling experts offer the following guidelines for first-responders, caregivers, family, and friends who will be in contact with the rape victim:

- **Believe her.** The greatest fear of acquaintance rape survivors is that they will not be believed or that their experience will be minimized.

- **Acknowledge that the rape was not her fault.** Avoid questions such as "Why did you go out with him?" that imply she is at fault for the assault. Allow her to talk out her feelings of self-blame if she wants to, but help her understand that the assailant was out of control and responsible for the act, not her.

- **Listen.** Let her know that you are there, whenever she wants to talk. Do not force her to talk until she is ready.

- **Help her organize her thoughts.** Allow her to make her own decisions about how to proceed. Remember that during the assault she had no control over what was happening to her. The acquaintance rape survivor needs to regain control. Trusting the victim to make the right decisions for herself can help her regain self-confidence.

- **Be available.** In the weeks and months that follow the rape, reassure her that she can turn to you whenever she needs to. Then, when she does, give her your undivided time and attention. Offering non-judgmental support and eliminating pressure can help. Give the victim some room to find her own emotions and needs, both physically and mentally.

- **Get help for yourself.** You may also need to talk to someone other than the acquaintance rape survivor to discuss your feelings about the attack and its aftermath.

Significant others become indirect victims of rape. They, too, may experience unexpected emotions. Anger, helplessness, and frustration are common and understandable reactions by those close to a sexual assault victim. These feelings are important and need attention, but should not override the needs of the victim. Rebuilding intimacies and trusting relationships takes time and effort on the part of everyone involved.

WHAT PROFESSIONALS CAN DO

It is important that caregivers and first-responders realize that after a sexual assault has been reported, police and medical professionals will need as much cooperation from the victim as possible. Well-trained, caring professionals will try to do this in a gentle manner without making the victim feel re-victimized. The following section will be helpful in understanding their actions and methods.

Law enforcement and medical personnel can also use this section to ensure that they are conducting themselves professionally and obtaining as much information as possible to facilitate apprehension and conviction of the perpetrator.

THE INTERVIEW

The interview should be conducted as soon as possible after the assault. The interviewer and family members can help the victim feel she is a part of the team that will locate and prosecute the suspect. Since many of the questions directly relate to the rape, the interview should be conducted in an environment where the victim feels secure. The victim's home may be more comfortable than the police department. The interviewer should be gentle and empathetic.

Law enforcement professionals today use new techniques called "profiling" for apprehending the suspect. In addition to gathering a detailed description of the suspect, they will also explore his behavior during the assault. For example, they will want to determine if the assailant lured the victim with kindness and tenderness preceding his mood and behavior shift.

Typical Investigative Questions

- **Perpetrator's description.** It is important that investigators get the most complete, detailed, description of the perpetrator possible. An investigator will ask if the perpetrator was masked or unmasked and if he wore glasses. Sometimes a police artist will be brought in to develop a composite sketch based on the victim's (or witnesses') description. Descriptive information includes the following:

  - Hair (head, facial, and body)
  - Facial features (eyes, ears, nose, mouth)
  - Distinctive marks
  - Hands
  - Clothing, shoes, jewelry
  - Odor

- **Physical behavior.** The interviewer will try to establish patterns of behavior leading to the attack, how the perpetrator acted during the attack, the level of physical violence demonstrated, nervousness, or characteristic mannerisms. He or she will also ask if there were any changes in this behavior during the contact.

82

- **Approach used to contact the victim.** The investigator will need to know whether the perpetrator overpowered the victim or used a deception to gain the victim's confidence.

- **Controlling the victim.** Questioning will establish how the perpetrator gained control over and restrained the victim, whether or not threats or physical force were used, and if any weapons were involved in gaining control.

- **Victim's resistance.** This information is relevant to the perpetrator's behavior. It is not the intent of police to second guess the victim's decision about offering resistance.

- **Perpetrator's escape.** Investigators will try to determine if the perpetrator's escape was planned or if it was an "afterthought." Other questions will regard a vehicle or other means of escape.

- **Souvenirs.** Often attackers will take a souvenir of the assault. It is important that the victim try to recall what she had in her possession at the time of the attack. She should check for missing underclothing, jewelry, shoes, and purse contents, especially pictures. The souvenirs that a perpetrator may take can be used as physical evidence later in the case. Although most perpetrators keep their souvenirs for a long period of time, sometimes they attempt to return them, which can be dangerous for their victims. Therefore, it is even more important that the victim be as forthright as possible about what was taken.

- **Verbal behavior.** Studying the perpetrator's accent, pattern of speech, tone of voice, and other verbal characteristics provides valuable clues that may lead to his apprehension. Investigators need to know the exact words the perpetrator used in his communication with the victim, and if the perpetrator had obtained the victim's name or other personal information before or during the attack.

- **Sexual behavior.** The victim must be as graphic and precise as possible about the attacker's demands and actions. It may be necessary for the interviewer to ask for clarification of the words used to describe the sexual behavior to be sure everyone involved is in agreement regarding their meaning. Many of these personal questions may be difficult for the victim because they necessitate reliving the crime.

- **Victim information.** Questions regarding the victim's normal activities, residence, habits, work, transportation, friends, and social routines assist investigators in finding and narrowing down potential suspects.

TELEPHONE HARASSMENT

The person on the other end of the telephone line using obscene language and making lewd suggestions may be a depraved individual, but most likely he is someone you would wave to on the street, or who wears a three-piece suit to the office, or who services your car. The perpetrator of telephone harassment may be young or old, wealthy or economically disadvantaged; but most likely, the perpetrator will be a male.

Whomever he is, he is emboldened by the anonymity of the telephone. Unseen and safely out of arm's reach, these perpetrators avoid the risks usually associated with the physical confrontation of crime. Because they are not endangered and they can seldom be apprehended, those who might not ordinarily commit a crime can clandestinely assault and exploit others using the telephone as their weapon. The perpetrator can select his victims at random—letting his fingers do the walking—any time, any place without personal risk to himself. He can assert aggressive, anti-social behavior with little fear of reprisal. The perpetrator may use the telephone to wage verbal war against another or as a vehicle for sadistic behavior.

Rampant crime and violence have made good teachers. We have learned not to open our doors until we know who is behind them. Yet, when the telephone rings, we don't think of ourselves as vulnerable, as a potential victim to an unseen perpetrator. Unsuspecting, we pick up the telephone and assume, or trust, that we are in control, that we are safe from invasion and violation.

The telephone has, for many of us, become our life-link. To cut ourselves off from family and friends, however temporarily, is unacceptable, and the perpetrator of telephone harassment uses our fear of isolation to her or his advantage.

The perpetrator's harassment is calculated to serve two purposes: to indulge in unacceptable behavior without fear of being identified; and to exert power over another by instilling fear or causing aggravation and anxiety. His actions can range from a brief episode of heavy breathing to lengthy, orchestrated contacts, during which he makes lurid, graphic remarks or engages his victim in exploitative conduct.

The most common form of telephone harassment incorporates lewd suggestions or descriptions, a kind of vicarious rape referred to as the "obscene" phone call.

It was 2 a.m. The phone startled Martin and Helen.

"Mr. Delacort? This is Officer Briggs from the police department. Your business has been broken into and we

need you to come down to determine if anything is missing.”

About five minutes after Martin had driven away, the phone rang again.

Mrs. Delacort? I'm not really a police officer. I have your husband at gun point, and if you don't do what I say, I'll kill him. Do you understand?”

Terrified, Helen believed the caller would kill her husband if she didn't do what he asked. For almost half an hour, he instructed her to disrobe and perform certain sexual acts. Repeatedly, he threatened her, saying he would know if she failed to do just as he said.

When Martin found that his business was intact, he became suspicious and called the police. No one had reported a break-in at his address, the dispatcher told him.

He rushed home, arriving moments after the caller had hung up. Helen was hysterical. It took him an hour to calm her enough to hear what had happened. The caller's violation of her, and his power over her, made her feel like she had been raped.

Though unnerved, most people who identify a call as obscene quickly hang up. For Helen, however, terminating the call was not an option. The caller convinced her that her husband's life was in jeopardy if she didn't do as he asked. In this way, the caller had successfully used fear to control and manipulate her behavior. Only her compliance, he had convinced her, would ensure her husband's safety.

In this respect, the telephone harassment Helen endured also made her a victim of sexual assault. Her reactions were intensified because she could not see or identify her assailant. Recovery would have been easier if she could have directed her anger at a real person rather than a faceless voice. Her assailant's anonymity further heightened her feelings of vulnerability and insecurity because she knew she would be unable to recognize him in a personal confrontation.

Most instances of telephone harassment are less devastating than Helen's. Perpetrators who single out their victims usually have some relationship to them, however distant. Their calls may be more aggravating than potentially dangerous.

While laws governing telephone harassment vary widely, victims should report such incidents to their local law-enforcement agency.

Caregivers, family, and friends can be supportive by allowing the victim to vent her or his feelings about the upsetting event.

CHAPTER VI

ASSAULT AND ROBBERY

Assault is the most common violent crime. Under this umbrella label are domestic assault, covered in Chapter IV, and sexual assault, described in Chapter V. Assault occurs frequently in robbery situations, or as an isolated incident in itself. This chapter describes typical reactions to assault and effective responses family, friends, and professionals can use.

McGillicutty's Tavern had been a busy place for a Thursday evening. Its two bartenders were barely able to keep up with the orders that kept four waitresses hopping. It was obvious to everyone that Joe was drunk.

"No more for you," Andy, the old bartender, told Joe when he ordered his fifth Scotch. Joe flashed the bartender a dirty look, then started yelling at him. When Andy wouldn't give in, Joe jumped over the bar and let his fist fly into the bartender's face. Andy hit the floor and Joe took the opportunity to kick him in the side. Before anyone could pull Joe off, he had punched Andy at least ten times and kicked him repeatedly.

It took Andy a week to recover well enough from his injuries to return to work. He had stitches over his right eye and a broken nose, which would always be a little crooked. Whenever he looked in a mirror, the little scar and the crook in his nose was a reminder of the night he made the mistake of doing his job and refusing to serve a drink to someone who was drunk.

ASSAULT VICTIMS' REACTIONS

Andy was the victim of aggravated assault. As in his case, nearly half of all reported assaults involve people who know each other. From the myriad of law, police, and detective programs on television, most Americans have heard the term aggravated assault and learned to associate it with personal injury. Legally, assault is any unlawful physical attack, which excludes self-defense. The attacker may or may not have used a weapon.

The severity of assaults varies, from minor confrontations to near-death situations. How frightening and how injurious the assault largely determines its emotional impact. Caregivers and professionals who understand how and why assault evokes strong feelings in its victims can best respond to them.

Assault victims report feelings and concerns that include:

- Anger or bitterness

- Realization of mortality

- Physical injury

- Medical bills

- Time lost from work

- Fear of reprisal

- Feeling betrayed if the assailant was a family member or friend

- Vulnerability

- Fear of driving if the victim was injured in a traffic accident

- Vulnerability if the assailant was motivated by jealousy
- Shame of losing control over the situation, or of being beaten

Anger or Bitterness

Andy knew Joe was drunk and out of control. Anyone who crossed him could have been his victim. Most victims, however, feel an attack is aimed specifically at them, and they take it personally. Their space, safety, and personal freedom have been violated. They suffer not only bodily injury, but also its financial and emotional repercussions.

Like many victims of assault, Andy lost income because he was temporarily unable to work. Time is also something victims lose. Time is lost for hospitalization, doctors' appointments, cooperating with law enforcement investigations, and following through with prosecutions within the legal system. No matter how minor the incident, assault disrupts the victim's routine and costs him time and money. Understandably, victimization makes people angry.

Anger directed at the assailant, where it is appropriately aimed, can motivate positive action, such as prosecution or development of street and neighborhood watch groups, and safer transport alternatives. However, being angry "at the system," "with society" or at other vague and amorphous entities serves no purpose and only adds to the victim's frustration. The best way to expunge anger is to prosecute the offender.

Realization of Mortality

A severely injured victim may not feel "lucky to be alive," regardless of how many people tell him that he is.

He may believe that at some point during the assault he was going to die. Anyone who is suddenly confronted with death gains a unique perspective on life, and the assault victim is no different. The strong psychological aspect of assault can and does change people's lives. Under normal, day-to-day conditions, most people feel immortal. They may not think of it is those terms, but, at the least, they do not expect to die in the immediate future. A serious assault can sharply focus an individual's attention on how quickly life can end.

Caregivers and first-responders can help the victim acknowledge his fear of death, or debilitating injury, and begin to feel safe again. The victim can be guided gently away from stressful thoughts and toward areas in his immediate life where he does have control. Gaining control, even over small matters, will ease the victim's fear of mortality.

Physical Injury and Medical Bills

Victims of assault may neglect getting the medical attention they need for several reasons. The first is denial. Dismissing or lessening the severity of their injuries has the emotional impact, at least temporarily, of short-circuiting feelings of vulnerability and consequence. In essence, when there are no injuries, there is no victim and no crime.

The other reason victims sometimes do not receive necessary medical attention is culpability. Who will pay for their hospitalization and other medical bills that accrue as he or she recovers from injuries received in the assault? This can be an added stress for those who are uninsured or underinsured. Hospital social service units will often work out reasonable arrangements for delayed or reduced payment for those who have difficulty meeting this sudden expense. In recent years, victim compensation programs have offered assistance with financial burdens imposed by victimization. The victim should always be encouraged to get the medical attention he needs. A medical assessment can determine if additional treatment is needed. Ignoring injuries may be more expensive in the long run.

Time Lost from Work

Many families do not have a nest egg to fall back on in the event its financial provider is out of work. When a family loses its primary income because of injuries from an assault, the stress on the family can ripple into all corners of their lives.

Caregivers and first-responders can help victims and their families search for resources and look for creative ways to earn income. Often, there are community groups or churches willing to adopt a family. Such intervention can help a family in crisis avert financial disaster. In many states, law enforcement agencies offer victim assistance programs. Families can also assess their individual skills and look to unconventional and creative income-producing opportunities.

Fear of Reprisal

If it happened once, it could happen again, think many victims of assault. Their feeling of vulnerability is increased if they have reported the crime. They may fear being a target of the perpetrator's retaliation. If these fears are justified, they may wish to seek police protection. If their fears are no more than a residual reaction to being assaulted, then counseling and therapy can help allay them, or put them into proper perspective.

Feeling Betrayed

For the victim of assault by a family member or friend the phrase, "who can you trust these days," takes on new meaning. Being betrayed by someone trusted inflicts a great psychological wound. The victim is likely to question his judgment of character and become skeptical and distrusting of people. The victim may also be put in the precarious position of finding it difficult to avoid contact with the assailant.

Fear of Driving

Automobiles have become an extension of our personalities. As some people take this attachment to the extreme, vehicular assault is becoming increasingly common. Immature and out-of-control drivers take their frustration out on anyone in their path. Their vehicle becomes a weapon, and they wield it with reckless disregard for the consequences. Vehicles are involved in assault indirectly as well. Almost daily we hear news reports that someone was shot or injured because she or he frustrated another driver in a traffic jam or accident.

It may be helpful to know that victims whose assault involved automobiles were not being singled out. Through no fault of their own, they just happened to be in the wrong place at the wrong time. A normal reaction is to fear driving or getting into peak traffic situations again. This will pass. If it does not, and the anxiety becomes acute, the victim should seek professional counseling.

Vulnerability

When an assault has been motivated by the assailant's jealousy, there is a strong possibility that the victim may fear additional reprisals or a potentially fatal attack. Jealousy is a powerful emotional trigger and should be taken seriously. The goal of law enforcement authorities and the victim should be protection through successful prosecution and conviction of the assailant.

Feeling Shame

Particularly when the assault occurred in the presence of a spouse or girlfriend, a male may convince himself that his victimization demonstrated that he is weak and ineffectual. His injuries may be painful, though irrational, reminders that he has lost face in front of someone whom he wished to impress.

Because an assault can rarely be anticipated, the victim is caught off guard, and the assailant has the advantage. Victims do not need to feel weak or inadequate because they could not overcome their assailant, especially when a weapon was involved. If feelings of inadequacy persist, however, victims should seek counseling to put the incident in a realistic perspective.

ROBBERY AND BURGLARY

Home is our sanctuary, our refuge. When intruders violate the sanctity that is our personal space, they violate us as well. They perpetrate a crime by invading our privacy and threatening our security. When they steal our possessions, burglars rob us of extensions of ourselves. We are not what we own. Yet what we own is an expression of who we are.

Robbery adds another dimension to that violation. We meet the offender in a risky confrontation. His threat and ultimatum put him in control. We may be assaulted or believe that we will be if we do not comply. We relinquish personal property and, for the moment, autonomy. Orderliness has been disrupted and we are out of balance.

Stickup, holdup, mugging, or robbery, whatever word is used, this most serious and frequent criminal offense conjures images of shadowy figures ready to leap at us from dark doorways. They instill fear that we will have our throats slashed for our pocket change.

Though our odds of being victimized in this way are small, time and place can increase them. Statistics support our common beliefs about robbery. More than half of robberies take place under the cover of darkness, a time when the greatest number of injuries occurs. One in 12 robbery victims experienced serious injuries such as rape, knife or gunshot wounds, broken bones, or being knocked unconscious, according to the National Crime Survey.

Almost nine out of ten robberies are committed by a male stranger. In slightly more than half of these, victims were physically attacked. As suspected, people 65 years of age and older were somewhat more likely to be attacked than those in other age groups. Females are injured more than males.

Occasionally, robbers encounter victims who are prepared to fight back, not with wit or brawn, but with weapons of their own. Thwarted robberies, of course, do occur. Yet, not surprisingly, three-fourths of reported attempts were successfully completed when the victim received injuries serious enough to send her or him to the emergency room.

The more serious the injury and the greater the property loss, the greater the likelihood the victim will report the robbery to authorities. Those who report the incident say they do so to protect themselves and others from having it happen again and to punish the offender.

Since both victims of burglary and robbery risk injury and have property stolen, they share similar feelings about their victimization. The most common reactions are listed below, along with resourceful ways first-responders can help victims deal with their feelings:

REACTION   **Fear of venturing into the street alone.** Depending on the circumstances of the robbery, the victim may make major changes in her lifestyle and curtail activities such as jogging or taking long walks alone.

RESPONSE   Provide the victim with safety information and suggest self-defense classes.

REACTION   **Frustration at the loss of personal effects.** Personal effects represent not only a monetary investment to the victim, but also an emotional investment Stolen property cannot be replaced overnight.

RESPONSE   Offer a robbery victim information on procedures for replacing driver's license, social security card, credit cards, and other important documents. Demonstrate understanding to the victim of burglary that personal effects, as an extension of the self, are irreplaceable, and represent memories and continuity to the past. Understand that the sentimental loss may be more devastating than the financial loss.

REACTION   **Feeling of violation.** Burglary victims may wonder, "If I cannot be safe in my own home, where can I be safe?"

RESPONSE   This is a valid concern. Offer suggestions for making the home more secure.

REACTION   **Reluctant to leave the home.** The victim may be fearful that his home will be burglarized again if he leaves.

RESPONSE   Suggest that installation of a home security device or system will enhance his feelings of security.

REACTION   **Reluctant to stay home.** The victim may fear another intrusion by the burglar and a dangerous confrontation.

RESPONSE   Suggest that installation of a home security device or system will enhance his feelings of security.

REACTION   **"If only I had...."** Hindsight may influence victims of burglary and robbery to perceive they could have prevented the incident.

RESPONSE   Stress to the victim that the burglary or robbery was not his fault. Demonstrate confidence that he now knows how to take precautions to reduce the risk of future victimization.

REACTION   **Distress over heavy financial losses.** The victim's home may have been stripped of valuables or vandalized, or he may have been robbed of jewelry, credit cards, or a significant amount of cash.

RESPONSE   Suggest he immediately report the theft of credit cards to respective card companies. If the theft occurred in his insured home, suggest that he place an immediate insurance claim. He may also be able to itemize for deduction as a casualty loss on his personal income tax return.

First-responders and caregivers can also assist the victim through the following actions:

• Channel the victim's anger in a positive direction.

• Acknowledge his feeling of isolation. Suggest he reach out to his neighbors, or initiate a neighborhood watch program.

• Explain the need for his full cooperation with law enforcement authorities.

• Suggest financial resources through community assistance programs to help secure the home.

CHAPTER VII

LOSING A LOVED ONE
TO SUDDEN DEATH

Adrian's pregnancy hadn't been particularly eventful. She, Brian and their 4-year-old, Sean, waited out the last six weeks before the baby's arrival painting and papering his room. The ultrasound exam looked good, and their new son appeared restless to meet his big brother.

When she went into labor four weeks early, Adrian was more relieved than alarmed. Brian grabbed her overnight case from the closet and before traffic peaked, they reached the admissions desk at St. Joseph's. Her obstetrician caught up with her wheelchair at the elevator on the sixth floor. Brian left her side only for those brief moments it took to prep her.

The next few hours changed his life. It had all seemed to go so fast. The decision to perform an emergency cesarean. The obstetrician's piercing words: "We're losing her." The beepings and oscillations of the monitors. This doesn't happen, he told himself. All this technology...women don't die in childbirth anymore.

Aaron's first cry echoed in his ears throughout Adrian's funeral. He pressed the sleeping red-headed bundle against his chest. He could feel his heart pound.

"What do I do now?" it seemed to beat out rhythmically. He had no answer. There was only the numbness.

SUDDEN DEATH AND GRIEVING

Death is inevitable. Intellectually, we know that; yet we act as if our lives, and the lives of those connected to us, continue forever.

The sudden, unexpected death of a loved one must be the sharpest pain of all. When someone dear to us suffers a long illness or is aging, we have time to prepare for her death. Occasionally, then more often, we begin to visualize what our lives will be like in her absence. The grieving can and does begin early. There is time to say good-bye. To say "I love you." "I remember the happy times." " I will miss you." When death closes the chapter on our shared lives, we accept its finality. What could be done has been.

When a loved one dies unexpectedly, however, friends and family are faced not only with the pain of loss, but also with myriad tasks and events resulting from the death. This chapter examines reactions to sudden deaths, such as homicide, suicide, accidents, and Sudden Infant Death Syndrome.

Death is, perhaps, the most abstract concept about living. Intellectually, we understand it as a continuum. We fear it or welcome it according to our religious and cultural conditioning. Mostly, we are removed from it. When someone close to us dies, however, our vague ideas of what death is become harsh reality. We long to come to terms with the life and death of the person who has left us behind.

Grieving is the process of reconciling sorrow. Through grief, we learn about ourselves and our ability to creatively go on with our lives, despite, or because of, the pain of our loss. We recognize the void for what it is. We come to terms with mortality.

Unlike many societies, ours expects the bereaved to "get over it" quickly. Mourners are allowed to publicly express their grief during the funeral period. Once the body is interred, family and friends who still demonstrate grief are viewed by some as weak, overly sensitive, or lacking strength and character.

Such expectations are unfortunate and inappropriate. It is not a simple matter of having a good cry and then it is over. Grieving can continue for years. We need to learn what other cultures have long acknowledged: grief is a therapeutic, personal act. Great and elaborate rituals have surrounded the mourning period. Protracted ceremony is a rite of passage for the living as much as a testimony to honor the dead.

The loss of a loved one alters the basic structure of family and relationships. It hurts. Those who expect recovery from the pain in a matter of days or weeks have not experienced the death of someone they care about. As we have seen in an earlier chapter, counselors who work with the grieving note that the mourning period is characterized by the following stages: shock, searching, disorganization, and readjustment. The emotions experienced at each of these stages are intensified when the death is sudden.

Our first reaction to sudden death is shock. Mourners aptly describe their condition as a state of disbelief. They are dazed. The news is so overwhelming and unacceptable that for self-protection our body automatically numbs our senses. The numbness gives us space and time to begin adjusting.

After a few days, the shock wears off. We begin to search for ways to hold on to the life and memory of the one who has died. This period is marked by much restless activity. We cling to their personal characteristics or possessions as if to confirm that our loved ones are still here.

The next stage may take longer. We, the survivors, realize that the deceased is not coming back. We enter a period of emotional disorganization. Survivors are likely to withdraw from regular routines and social contacts.

It is during this time that the burden of loss and feeling of hopelessness may lead to depression. Or, out of frustration and a sense of powerlessness, survivors may become angry. Their anger may be directed to the one who has died ("How could he leave me?"), to doctors ("You should have saved him."), God ("What did I do to deserve this?"), or themselves ("I should have.... I shouldn't have....").

The final phase of grieving is one of acceptance. This occurs when survivors begin to readjust their lives. Survivors ask, "Where do I go from here?" and "What do I do now?" These questions mark turning points in their lives. Survivors are looking to the future, rather than reliving the past.

Common Reactions During Grieving

It *is* normal for the grieving process to take one to three years. What is behaviorally inconsistent for those who are not mourning may be quite normal for those who are. Among the common reactions to the death of someone close are:

• Signs of emotional distress indicated by such physical symptoms as headache, upset stomach, loss of appetite, shortness of breath, tightness of the throat, dizziness, and constant fatigue

• Talking about the person in present tense, rather than past tense

• Visual and auditory hallucinations by which the survivor sees or hears the person who has died

• Preoccupation with thoughts of the dead loved one and death itself

• Nervousness, with no readily apparent cause

- Anxiety about the future

- Feelings of not wanting to live or not being able to live any longer

- Feelings of disorientation, self-doubt, questions about going crazy
- Withdrawing from others

- Feeling envious of those who have not suffered the loss

- Idealizing the deceased loved one

How Survivors Can Help Themselves

The most important thing survivors need remember is that the expression of grief is necessary. In time, it enables us to form new relationships and discover new and creative ways to design our lives. Grief counselors advise survivors to keep the following in mind:

- Friends and family will *give* you their support, but they also need to *receive* it. Talk with them, hold them, and try not to withdraw.

- Expect stress on your marriage relationship and relationships with your children. If your family is already stressed, seek a support group. Call your local hospital, health department, or mental health center. The loss of a child often results in parental separation or divorce. Don't attempt to "go it alone." Ask for help.

- If friends ask you how you're doing, don't say, "fine," and then get angry because you have no one to talk to about your grief. Tell them, honestly, what you're feeling.

- Don't accept "advice" or expressions of concern that are nonconstructive or make you angry. Say what's on your mind. Stick up for yourself.

- Don't be surprised if people you thought were your friends stop calling. Death and grief are too much for some people to cope with.

- Experts recommend that you do not move so quickly as to "forget the past." There will be time to "make a new start." Hasty escapes only further disrupt family lives. Memories must include good times. Abandoning your home is much like abandoning the life and love of the one who has died. Grief counselors advise against making any major changes in your life during the first year of grief.

- Many survivors attest to the benefits of keeping a journal. It is easier to express in writing thoughts that come with great difficulty verbally. Journals are both an outlet and a testimony to where you've been.

Helping Someone Else Through Grief

Most of us aren't confident that we'll say the right things to someone who has just experienced the loss of a loved one. So, we say nothing, or nothing meaningful. The survivor, cued by our silence and awkwardness, is unsure of how or when to express his feelings. So, he says nothing. Two people who could offer each other support and comfort are left in silence, hurting, angry, feeling guilty.

The greatest gift you can offer a grieving friend is your willingness to listen. Your mission isn't to talk to make things better. Your mission is to listen. Don't discount his feelings or pretend they don't exist.

"You'll get over this," or, "A brighter day is coming" are empty words to the person in pain over a death. Trite phrases tell a mourner to leave you alone and go bother someone else. As a greeting card company implies, "...when you care enough to send the very best," your extra efforts show where your heart is.

Don't be afraid to say, "This must be terribly hard for you," and allow her to tell you earnestly how hard it is. She can't work through her grief unless she experiences it. You don't have to say anything. You don't even have to provide any answers. Seeing how you comfort her through loving support, valuing her feelings, demonstrates how she can comfort and nurture herself.

Let him cry. While crying may upset you or the people around you, those who are grieving need to shed tears. Changing the subject will not make the pain go away. Telling someone to, "Be brave. Chin up. You'll be all right," only encourages him to dwell with his grief alone and out of your sight.

Your attitude and caring actions always speak louder than words. Here are some suggestions:

• Immediately after the death, don't say, "Call me if I can help with anything." Do something. Make a meal. Mow a lawn. Offer your car or home to out-of-town relatives. Volunteer to stay with the children, pets, or elderly relatives while funeral arrangements are being made or services are being held.

• After the funeral, don't assume your friend needs time to be alone and "work things out," or that grieving is exclusively a "family matter." Being alone may be the last thing he needs. Make yourself available. Don't wait for him to reach out.

- If your friend declines your offer of dinner or conversation and says, "There's nothing more anyone can do," accept the magnitude of the pain and don't press. Remember that grief is a process, not a permanent state. Ask again later.

- Don't be afraid to talk about the person who died, not about their death, but about their life.

- You may feel that because you have not experienced the death of someone close that you have nothing of value to offer your friend in his time of sorrow. You're wrong. You're a witness to the grief and a means for the survivor to grow through it. Share your doubts and fears. In this way you will extend your friendship, not end it.

HOMICIDE

For millennia, we have known the power of the human touch to heal. Perhaps this is one of the reasons why we find it altogether unfathomable that death can come to someone we love at the hands of another. Deliberately, coldly.

As youngsters, we flourished in the sublime security of a familiar environment. Entrusted to the care of those who loved us, we were out of harm's way. Over time, we were exposed to a less-than-trustworthy world, and our perceptions of invulnerability began to shift. Graphically, we were confronted with examples of malicious human intent. It was sobering. Forever after, we are changed. Our thoughts and actions reflect the interpersonal nature of crime and violence in our society. We are disillusioned to find the world a perilous place.

We are more than our bodies and minds. We are interpersonal beings. When a wrongful act has severed our relationship with someone close to us, threads within the fabric of our being unravel.

Homicide is a doubly cruel act. Survivors must first cope with the shock caused by the sudden death of a loved one. For years thereafter their remembrances of his life will be associated with his violent death. Additionally, survivors' pain is further complicated and burdened by a police investigation, the criminal justice system, medical and funeral expenses, the media, and even by reactions of friends, and family. The strain and demands may affect survivors' job attendance and performance, studies, and relationships with others. When it does, professional counseling is beneficial in dealing with the stress and grief.

Two of three homicide categories—murder and non-negligent, or voluntary, manslaughter—are defined as the willful killing of one human being by another. In the third category, negligent, or involuntary, manslaughter, intent to kill is absent. In some instances, one person unintentionally, or recklessly, causes the death of another. One example is a death caused by a drunk driver.

According to the Uniform Crime Report's most recent statistics, approximately three-fourths of the victims willfully killed by another were male. One-third were between the ages of 20 and 29. As in cases of domestic violence, many victims knew each other. In nearly one-tenth of all reported cases, one spouse killed the other.

Drug-related crimes, sexual assault, and robbery accounted for 18 percent of murders and non-negligent manslaughter.

Regardless of the manner of death, the loss of human life is no less tragic. Yet, for friends, family, co-workers, even schoolmates, the emotional consequence differs greatly. In order to communicate effectively with these individuals, first-responders, law enforcement officers, counselors, and others need to understand that, in addition to shock and confusion, survivors may demonstrate:

- **Preoccupation with any suffering the victim may have experienced.** Survivors may want to know details of the victim's death. In cases where the details are grotesque or where torture was involved, it is wise to discuss the best method of sharing this information with a trained counselor. Use common sense in answering these questions.

- **Increased emphasis on day-to-day routines.** This may be a coping strategy to help them feel more secure.

- **Insomnia, flashbacks, nightmares,** and other physical and emotional signs of stress.

- **Fear.** Depending on the circumstances of the victim's death, survivors may fear for their own safety.

- **Hostility and anger.** Survivors may lash out at others because they recognize no one can bring the victim back into their lives.

- **Hopelessness.** Experiencing the void in their lives is painful. They may become depressed or feel guilty that they did not somehow protect the victim and prevent the homicide.

SUICIDE

Today, many psychologists consider suicide more a behavior than an act of self-destruction. It is a subject much on our minds and much in the news. In the last year alone, numerous documentaries and educational programs have focused on an increasing number of suicides—especially among the young—assisted suicide, and death with dignity. Spotlights on this psychosocial phenomenon make more poignant our struggle to answer one of our toughest questions: Do we have the right to say when and how we will die?

Consider that every action of our life is programmed for survival. We are trained, urged, coaxed, rewarded to be well-adjusted, well-adapted to life. We cling to life through sickness, accident, war. Despite our travails, we awake with a zest for the new dawn. The laughter of a baby restores us. We learn to give and take, roll with the punches. Suicide seems like the bottom of the roller coaster.

To people shouldering unbearable stress, however, the opportunity for relief is welcoming. Sometimes silently they plead with us: "Please listen. Know our suffering."

When a loved one takes her own life, we feel not her pain, but ours, and perhaps, excruciating guilt for not recognizing hers.

A suicide, like other forms of sudden death, leaves survivor-victims. Parents, children, siblings, friends, other relatives, and co-workers all must find their individual and appropriate ways to work through their grief and feelings about the death. Survivors can expect to experience a range of emotions through the various stages of recovery.

Shock

Because we don't anticipate it, suicide is a shock. We react with numbness. Unlike the shock experienced for other types of sudden death, the impact is intensified if survivors have observed the suicide or if they have been the ones who found the body. If the victim chose to die violently, the trauma is exacerbated.

Shock gives way to a myriad of other emotions.

Guilt

Survivors quickly reflect on the suicide victim's most recent behavior, groping for mental clues that might have revealed his intent. Guilt floods in, whether or not the behavioral clues could be identified. The "what-if" game begins. "What if I had not been too busy to talk with him yesterday?" "What if I had not yelled at her when we were disagreeing?" "What if I had spent more time with him when he needed me?" "What if we could have accepted his homosexuality?"

"What if?" is counterproductive.

Those outside the survivors' immediate circle may unwittingly, or deliberately, brand survivors with guilt. "Why didn't you see the signs?" "What was going on in your family that he couldn't deal with anymore?"

"Why didn't you?" is counterproductive.

Survivors confronted by judgmental or insensitive co-workers, friends and neighbors may find it beneficial to rehearse a response based on what they have learned about suicide from this book. Or pass this book along.

Guilt is one way our conscience prods us awake, alerts us to the need to be better prepared. It can facilitate hope—if we do not let it mire us in doubt.

Bewilderment

Bewilderment and confusion can overcome survivors who struggle with the reasons for their loved one's decision to die. Even those who are not debilitated by guilt search for answers. Perhaps the best recourse is acceptance that understanding is not an intellectual exercise, a rationalization of pros and cons to be meted out in two neat columns. Rather, it is a joining of the heart. What *can* be understood is that the loved one felt extraordinary pain longer than she could endure. We don't have to approve. We don't have to flail ourselves because we didn't see or hear the warnings. We need only be sensitive to the pain in others.

Recovering

Survivors entering the grief process need reassurance that their feelings are valid if recovery is to be complete. Communicating these feelings to others through support groups for survivors of suicide victims is particularly helpful. Within the folds of the noncondemning support group, they are welcome, secure that they are not alone. Here, nurturing and growth can take place.

Caregivers, first-responders, or law enforcement personnel who announce the sad news to the family can help provide them with direction and advise them of steps that now need to be taken. Additional helpful actions include:

- Encourage survivors to say "good-bye" to the loved one. Caregivers or law enforcement personnel should prepare them for what they will see and accompany them to the hospital or morgue.

- Recommend the family proceed with burial as with any death.

- Suggest the obituary simply read the person "died at home."

- Reinforce to the family that the victim's death was clearly a choice.

SUDDEN INFANT DEATH SYNDROME (SIDS)

Babies are promise, hope, and future. When an infant with no history of life-threatening illness dies suddenly, inexplicably in her crib, SIDS is usually suspected. Sudden Infant Death Syndrome is both unpredictable and unpreventable. It is the leading cause of death for infants after the first week of life. Annually, 6,000-8,000 tiny lives are lost to this mysterious death, involving families in all social and economic levels.

For reasons researchers are still struggling to explain, infants are most at risk for "crib death" in their first six months of life, especially during winter and early spring.

Cause of death is not suffocation, aspiration, regurgitation, or genetic. A minor illness, such as a cold, may precede death, but most infants who die suddenly show no observable symptoms. As multiple factors contribute to death, no single test can yet determine an infant's risk.

SIDS deaths usually occur during sleep, and parents may not discover the death until morning or at the end of nap time. As a result, many parents suffer unwarranted guilt and seriously question their child-rearing abilities.

Because death investigations are often handled in the same manner as a homicide, it is important that the family understand each step of the process. In some states, an autopsy may be required. Although it may be difficult to consider, an autopsy may actually reassure parents that their infant's death was not the result of negligence on their part. Where an autopsy is not required by law, parents may wish to consult with their family physician to confirm the cause of death.

First-responders and caregivers can expect a range of behaviors from parents that include shock, self blame, numbness, rage, and hysteria. They can assist the family through thoughtful responses such as:

- Expressing condolences

- Informing parents that their baby did not suffer

- Arranging transportation for the family or absent parent

- Listening to their feelings of sorrow and frustration

- Avoiding judgmental statements that minimize the importance of the child, such as, "At least you have other children"

- Being willing to touch

- Accepting their reactions

- Providing information about their local SIDS Program

CHAPTER VIII

DISASTERS

Floods, earthquakes, tornadoes, hurricanes, major fires, transportation accidents, acts of terrorism, all take enormous tolls on lives and resources. The magnitude of human and material losses wreaks havoc on individual and group emotional and financial stability. Disasters are crises of the most severe proportion. Man-made or natural, in seconds, minutes, they create a "community" of victims and bring out the worst and the best in people.

In crisis, leaders emerge, victims bond with others who have shared the life-and-death experience. Initial disunity is mobilized into community. Cohesion peaks during a disaster, but so, too, do stress, tension, and the drain on medical, law enforcement, and government resources.

Each person is unique and tolerates the stress of a disaster based on their various coping strategies and experiences. Stress is most severe, of course, when it threatens life or limb rather than property alone. The person with a reliable support system—family, friends, community—is better equipped to cope successfully with stress than the person who goes through the crisis experience alone.

Disaster victims react to severe stress in one of three ways. They may become unusually quiet and emotionally paralyzed, suddenly hysterical, or appear calm and remain relatively functional.

Emotionally paralyzed victims may wander aimlessly, or appear dazed and immobile. Caregivers need to be alert for the symptoms of shock, such as nausea, shallow breathing, weak pulse, and dizziness. Beneath the silent, subdued exterior rages a tumultuous psychological storm. These victims should be removed to calmer surroundings where they feel safe and secure. When this is not possible, volunteers can help prevent further emotional distress by blocking or limiting their visual exposure to graphic scenes.

Hysterical victims are the most dangerous to themselves, caregivers, and others. Their reaction can be contagious and disrupt the efforts of others to organize rescue activities. Even when no injury is apparent, the hysterical person should be transported to a medical facility. Caregivers also can designate volunteers to remove him from the scene and remain with him until emergency personnel take over. Hysterical victims usually respond to direct, firm commands to perform specific helping tasks, which enable them to focus on something other than themselves and to regain control.

Some disaster victims are inherently able to ignore their own needs and remain functional. It is not unusual to find them assisting with rescue efforts. These victims are not unaffected by their trauma. They have merely put their stress reaction on hold. Caregivers should make every effort to observe their behavior for signs of physical and emotional overload.

In general, victims' immediate, or short-term, reactions to disasters include shock, confusion, preoccupation with pain and suffering, as well as a preoccupation with inexplicable loss.

Over the coming months or years, as disaster victims struggle to reorganize their lives, they may experience a host of reactions such as: flashbacks and nightmares, withdrawal, separation anxiety, feelings of isolation or estrangement, anger and hostility, fear, depression, apathy, disillusionment, helplessness, and hopelessness.

Children are particularly vulnerable to the effects of disasters. Their small world was a familiar, predictable, safe place where bad things seldom happened and, when they did, someone was there to protect them. Disasters, however, are events that seem unreal and dreamlike. Their scope is often beyond even adult comprehension. They stagger the mind with their enormity and turn lives inside out.

For children, the experience is magnified by their inability to verbalize the emotional upheaval going on inside them. Even children who are normally independent and fearless become terrified when they see and sense the terror in adults.

That doesn't mean adults should hide their fears. It is possible to demonstrate personal strength and simultaneously express anxieties. More important than whether or not one is fearful is overcoming the fear, or at least, not allowing the fear to be debilitating. For adults and children, openly sharing emotions in an atmosphere of love and acceptance can diminish anxiety and encourage healing.

Statements such as, "It was a scary feeling," "I know you were afraid," and "It's natural to be afraid," are non-condemning and open pathways for dialogue. They are permission-giving and allow for further and deeper expression. Seeing adults work through fear to solve problems teaches children positive coping mechanisms and heightens their sense of security.

Young children who have internalized the traumatic event may reenact its most terrifying moments in a melodramatic or even playful way. Caregivers who understand the benefits of this play-acting will allow it to run its course rather than dismiss it as harmful.

The apprehensive child who is waiting for the next shoe to drop is demonstrating her insecurity. She may withdraw and revert to infantile behavior, such as sucking her thumb and rocking herself to sleep. She may also wake up repeatedly during the night and need reassurance that her family will still be there in the morning to take care of her. Aggressive behavior during this time often signals the need for nurturing and positive reinforcement. This is a time for love and touching, not for discipline.

When parents and caregivers discount or dismiss his fears as unfounded, the child feels rejected, ashamed, unloved, or unprotected. These feelings feed his fear. During this critical time, caregivers can offer the child emotional tools to cope with daily stress and gain the confidence needed to become an independent adult.

Caregivers and parents can demonstrate sensitivity through the following responses:

- Approach the child slowly.

- Crouch to the child's eye level.

- Call the child by name.

- Find out if she/he has a physical support that is missing (doll, stuffed animal, blanket) and may be found. Ask its name and how the child relates to the security object.

- Tell the child what you are going to do before you do it.

- Bring the family together as quickly as possible.

- Urge parents to take their children with them during errands, appointments, and other important activities after the disaster.

Children who are included get the message, "We are still together. Our house, car, pets are gone, and that is sad, but we are together, safe, and we love you." Children who are involved in putting their family's world back in order feel reassured that someone is in control. In seeing the range of necessary tasks that follow, they come to understand something of the efforts their parents are making to restore unity. They learn critical problem-solving skills as well.

As death from any cause is a difficult concept to grasp, younger children will need help in dealing with it. Children associate death with abandonment, and it is being deserted that they fear most. Older children may be afraid the event will happen again or that they may die. Adults can be more objective in their assessment of recurrent danger; but the child's fearful state and immaturity preclude such understanding. A child's imagined dangers loom as real as the dreaded monster that lurks in the shadows of his room.

Parents and caregivers should encourage children exposed to death to talk about it. With love and support, they are tough and resilient. Loss of a parent or sibling, grandparent or friend leaves a scar, but helps a child understand that death is part of the cycle of life. A child who shares in the experience of his parents' grief learns compassion and that people are treasures to be cherished.

Children react to death in much the same way as adults. They experience denial, guilt, and anger or may be obsessed with thoughts that the dead person will come back.

- **Denial.** A child can be melodramatic or casual, pretending he is unaffected by the loss. He may even say he doesn't want to talk about it.

- **Guilt.** She may ask how she can be alive when he is dead. She may feel responsible.

- **Anger.** He may direct his anger at anyone, including the person who abandoned him.

Most children want to know what it is like to be dead. Following are some suggestions for talking about death and dying:

- Talk about death as permanent, without euphemisms. Dead people are not asleep. They do not wake up, breathe, eat, or drink.

- It's OK to say, "I don't know."

- Don't be surprised if your child does not appear to be grieving. She may believe she has to control her feelings. Give her permission to tell you she hurts.

- It's OK to evoke sad feelings and tears. Losing a loved one *is* sad. Crying is therapeutic. Let the child grieve in her own way, however, not yours.

- Encourage the child to remember the good things about the person who has died.

- When a child wants to set a place at the table for a dead parent or sibling, be firm, but gentle. You can say, "Mommy isn't coming back. She is dead, and we have to help each other accept that."

Rest and relaxation are viable ways to reduce stress. Even the demands of a disaster should not prohibit families from sharing quiet, restorative moments that re-energize them for the tasks ahead. But families should avoid prolonged inactivity that can become immobilizing. Doing *something* is making progress. It helps everyone to restore routines, or make new ones appropriate to the surroundings. Families who create a game or ritual out of mundane activities make light work of their tasks and ease their emotional burden.

When parents' best efforts fail to alleviate their child's anxiety, professional help is a wise choice. The key to its long-term effectiveness is prompt attention. Caregivers and parents can call their pediatrician, family physician, or local mental health center for referrals.

Sometimes we are forewarned about impending danger and whole communities are ordered to evacuate their homes. Leaving a familiar surrounding during a time of crisis adds stress to an already terrifying situation. Adults and children will experience fear, anxiety, and tension during a disaster evacuation. Separated from familiar and safe surroundings they become disoriented and confused. Stress is compounded if they are temporarily separated from loved ones.

Caregivers and first-responders should be especially sensitive to victims who are torn from their homes and crowded into community shelters or makeshift evacuation centers. Most people are social animals. Yet the lack of personal space, the absence of familiar objects, and the loss of privacy all contribute to their trauma. Whenever possible, allow victims to bring along some small, personal object that marks their temporary space their own.

Disasters indiscriminately snuff out lives, destroy property, and leave in their wake untold suffering. Approximately 140,000 Americans die each year from injuries received during catastrophes or other unexpected occurrences, making injury the fourth leading cause of death, just behind heart disease, cancer, and stroke. More than 80,000 victims each year receive permanently disabling injuries of the brain or spinal cord.

During a medical emergency, trained and untrained first-responders must act quickly and decisively to seek aid for the injured and prevent additional injury. A call for help is always a wise first move when emergency units are within responding distance. Properly applied, first aid may mean the difference between life and death. First aid, however, does not take the place of proper medical treatment.

Those who want to obtain first-aid, rescue breathing, or CPR (cardiopulmonary resuscitation) training should contact their local National Safety Council or the National Safety Council First Aid Training Agency for a listing of authorized courses in their community.

The National Safety Council advises that once responders have surveyed the scene for hazards, they need to assess whether or not life, limb, or major psychological damage is imminent. In addition to direct observation, caregivers can ask the victim if she needs medical attention. A victim in shock may either not respond or may respond inappropriately. She may experience high anxiety, hysteria, faintness, blackouts, disorientation, nausea, dizziness, or tingling in the fingers and toes, which can mask symptoms of serious injuries. Severe bleeding, seizures, and suspected respiratory or cardiac arrest all require immediate medical attention.

If the victim is conscious, those trained to provide first aid should always obtain consent to do so beforehand. First-responders untrained in first aid and CPR can still be valuable assistants to trained rescuers. The National Safety Council suggests they can:

- Go for help.

- Check the victim's breathing and pulse following directions from a trained rescuer.

- Assist or relieve an exhausted rescuer in CPR, following directions from a trained rescuer.

First-responders to a disaster will encounter a range of victim injuries and reactions. The following general guidelines help reduce the risk of additional injuries or deaths:

- Assess the situation.

- Designate a volunteer to call for help.

- Rescue victims in life-threatening situations.

- Reassure victims that help is on the way.

- Designate volunteers to assist injured victims.

- Calm hysterical victims or remove them from the scene.

- Avoid letting survivors become overly involved in rescue efforts.

- Designate a volunteer to create a list of victims.

- Reunite families as quickly as possible away from areas of greatest impact.

Assess the situation. Assessment of the scene will help first-responders determine what types of rescue efforts and resources are needed for an emergency response.

Designate a volunteer to call for help. Designating a specific bystander ("Sir, you in the blue jacket....") to call for assistance saves time, misunderstanding, and underscores urgency. It is more effective than an open request for "someone" to call 911. The caller must be ready with specific and detailed information about the emergency and be prepared to remain on the line with the dispatcher until she has all the necessary information. First-responders are often more effective remaining at the scene to coordinate activities until additional help arrives.

Rescue victims in life-threatening situations. To prevent further casualties, first-responders and volunteers must quickly assess whose lives are in immediate danger and move these victims out of harm's way.

Reassure victims that help is on the way. Designate volunteers to assist injured victims. Even untrained bystanders can provide injured victims with blankets, a calming, soothing voice, and a hand to hold. Minutes can seem like hours for a person alone in physical and emotional pain. The reassuring presence of someone who cares fills the victim with hope and facilitates his recovery.

Calm hysterical victims or remove them from the scene. Hysteria feeds upon itself and counters the efforts of restoring control to a crisis situation. As soon as possible, hysterical victims should be given prompt medical attention as their emotional reaction may mask injuries not readily observable. At the least, they should be taken to less-threatening surroundings, where efforts to calm them can be more successful.

Avoid letting survivors become overly involved in rescue efforts. Some survivors "need" to help as a defense mechanism from emotional breakdown. But because their physical and emotional capacity to cope with stress has been strained to the maximum by the impact of the crisis, they should be relieved as quickly as possible. Acknowledge their efforts and heroism and show they are appreciated.

Designate a responsible volunteer to create a list of victims and reunite families as quickly as possible away from areas of greatest impact. Medical personnel and law-enforcement authorities will compile official injury and casualty lists. In the meantime, anxious family and friends will be grateful for accurate information that their loved one is waiting for them in the lobby, or is en route to a specific hospital.

Separation from loved ones adds to victims' stress. When reunions are not immediately possible, relaying messages between victims and families can help reduce the stress and enable all concerned to make informed choices.

Dealing with death, especially for someone confronting it for the first time, is traumatic. Most people feel at a loss for the right thing to say or do. Most likely, the greatest gift anyone can give a dying person is their caring presence, assurance he is not alone, his loved ones are safe, and that someone will convey his love to them. Beyond this intuitive action, caregivers can:

- **Be respectful.** The dying person is a human being, someone's father, mother, son, or daughter.

- **Listen intently.** His words may mean nothing to the caregiver but everything to a loved one. Remember to convey them as accurately as possible.

- **Touch.** Touch is the gift of healing and love, the spiritual and physical connection between living things. It says to him he is not alone.

As soon after the initial impact of a disaster as possible, encourage victims to:

- Drink plenty of liquids.
- Balance rest with regular, appropriate exercise.
- Eat nutritious meals.
- Get plenty of restorative sleep.
- Avoid alcohol and drugs.
- Express grief.

Sometimes, caregivers make it a point to stay in touch with victims and their families. Their ongoing concern assures victims that they haven't been abandoned during the recovery process. Victims are more capable of restoring balance when they know they have support.

Here are other helpful tips that empower victims to take an active role in their reintegration and strengthen their emotional and physical selves:

- Practice rhythmic breathing, slowly and deeply for a few minutes to reduce tension. Victims can also benefit from meditation or relaxing thoughts.

- Understand no one can change the past. Worry won't make the future brighter. Planning for the future is more positive and productive than having expectations about it that may not be realistic.

- Look at the crisis as a collection of smaller problems. Work toward one solution at a time rather than approach the whole as a major catastrophe that seems overwhelming.

- Accept the assistance or advice of family and friends when it seems appropriate. Whining is tedious and alienates people.

- Release hostility and anger. Recognize them, transform them into problem-solving energy. Then let them go.

- Devote some time to activities that promote both physical and emotional health, such as walking, running, aerobics, swimming, or biking.

- Stick as closely as possible to a normal daily routine that provides structure and orderliness.

- Avoid strenuous mental and physical activity just before bedtime. Relaxing an hour or two before going to bed, or taking a walk, helps ensure more restful sleep.

- Take control of areas in your immediate life when and where you can.

Beyond personal injury and damage to property, disasters affect the livelihood of individuals and families. Income may be affected because time is lost from work. To date, there is little short-term (one to six weeks) financial assistance available for victims. Community groups may help prevent long-term financial distress by adopting individuals and families who are awaiting state or federal aid that is slow in materializing.

As time progresses and victims see their medical, relocation, or reconstruction bills mount, stress may build as well. Uninsured or underinsured victims are particularly hard hit by escalating expenses associated with disasters. Caregivers can help them arrange deferred or reduced payments with hospital social service units. Law-enforcement agencies can provide information regarding victim compensation programs.

There are as many ways caregivers can offer assistance as there are human needs. Additional thoughtful actions include:

- Protecting any remaining property at the victim's home

- Locating a short-term shelter

- Bringing food, clothing, bedding

- Providing transportation or a temporary vehicle

- Taking children to school or to participate in their usual extra-curricular activities

- Picking up and delivering mail to a relocation site

- Helping the victim replace important documents, such as driver's license, credit cards, birth certificate, marriage license, or social security card

- Videotaping extent of damage to property

- Identifying and listing destroyed items

- Assisting with processing of insurance claims and casualty loss statements for the Internal Revenue Service

Like children, the elderly are particularly devastated by a disaster. Feeling secure again is an uphill struggle. But unlike children, emotional and physical recovery are more of a challenge. Bones are brittle. Healing takes longer. The elderly need assistance but are reluctant to ask for it. They want to be treated with dignity and respect. They do not want to be treated as children.

For uninsured and underinsured elderly, whose financial resources already may be strained, mounting medical and relocation expenses create a tremendous hardship. Yet, the financial and physical impact of the disaster may be less devastating than the emotional.

Keepsakes and memorabilia are to older people links to the past and continuity with the future. Personal and family treasures are cues to memories. Their loss threatens day-to-day security. While such items cannot be replaced, caregivers can be sensitive to the void their loss creates. Bringing small personal gifts of significance to the individual goes a long way toward restoration and healing.

Since humans and animals first shared the warmth of a fire in clammy caves, they have been drawn to each other for companionship. Studies of the last decade have demonstrated the benefits to older citizens of owning a pet, or pet visitations. However, before bringing a kitten or puppy as a gift to an older person, be sure he or she is physically capable of accepting responsibilities for its training and care—including expenses.

Caregivers who take the initiative to assist an elderly individual can evaluate his needs in the context of his personal history.

CHAPTER IX

ELDERLY VICTIMS

Much of this country's elderly grew up in a time and place vastly different from the fast-paced, high-tech environment that confounds them today. Those who weren't reared in the city knew a world that was a quiet, rural expanse of families linked by fields and fences. It was a time when farmers and townsfolk never bothered to lock their doors. Neighbors were good, honest folks to be trusted. Young and old could safely walk the streets at night, and families looked out for one another.

As Bob Dylan's words rang out, "The times, they *are* a changin.'" And, indeed, technology has escalated change at a rate faster than in any previous half century.

Like electrons revolving around the nucleus of an atom, violence—urban and domestic—crime and family disenfranchisement seem inseparable from our contemporary society. As a result, today's elderly are particularly vulnerable to scams, fraud, and deception.

The face of America is aging. Since 1900, the average American has added 35 years to his longevity. By the year 2000, more than half of our population will be older than 50. A great proportion will be 85 and older. As numbers of the elderly increase, so does their potential for victimization.

According to the American Association of Retired Persons, "a third of people age 75 and older are classified in the high vulnerability category." Its recent survey cites the most common complaints as "products that didn't work, late deliveries, false or misleading claims, and bills for repairs far exceeding written estimates."

If it were only so simple. Exploitation of the elderly is not limited to deception and fraud, however. Like children, they are easy prey for assault, neglect, and abuse. As with children, many elderly are vulnerable because they are physically, emotionally, or financially dependent.

A 1989 study by Wolf & Pillemar shows that almost half of elderly victims used a cane, wheelchair, or walker. Even those who are relatively healthy and active and who have retained their independence are less able to resist attack and defend themselves than the next younger generation.

While the frequency of elder abuse is just slightly lower than that of child abuse, only one in 14 cases comes to the attention of authorities.

The mere fact that there are many more elderly people is not a satisfactory statistical explanation for the increase in elder abuse. To better understand this complex problem, we need to look at the social context from which this phenomenon emerges. Factors that enter into the equation and add up to increased vulnerability for our oldest citizens include:

- Families, professionals, and caregivers have limited knowledge of the physiology and psychology of the aging process.

- Families have little or no frame of reference for caring for the elderly.

- Insufficient support services are available to assist caregivers of the elderly.

- Hospitalization and drug costs are skyrocketing.

- Increased divorce rates produce single-parent families who may be struggling to rear children and can ill afford the financial responsibility of an older family member.

- Nuclear families are geographically scattered.

- Elder care lasts longer than child rearing, and its demands typically increase over time rather than decrease.

NEGLECT

Marjorie had been a nurse for forty-three years. Now, at 85, she lived alone in a ramshackle house that had been home for half a century. Most folks on her block could barely feed their families, much less repair their roofs and patch their porches. Her house looked little different from the rest.

When Marjorie's next door neighbor realized he hadn't seen her in nearly a week, he went over to check on her. He found her in bed. From the stench in her room, he knew she had not moved in days. He asked if she was all right, and she responded incoherently.

"Don't leave my pigeons," she whispered. "Don't leave my pigeons."

Within moments, the police, fire department, and paramedics had arrived. It was easy to see that Marjorie had sequestered herself in a corner of her little bedroom, turning over the rest of her house to at least two dozen pigeons that came and went through a broken window. Their billing and cooing kept her company. She fed them what she should have eaten. They were her treasures, and she took care of them, even if no one took care of her. They had become her family.

In big cities across the country, on lonely, rundown farms, even in convalescent care facilities, other Marjories suffer from abandonment, neglect, and abuse. Whether it is active or passive—an act of omission or of commission—inadequate care of the elderly is a national disgrace and should be a national concern. The elderly suffer needlessly from malnutrition, fractures, and other serious health problems that, left unattended, lead to death.

In some cultures status is associated with age. In this culture, where individual worth is tendered by productivity, advanced age is a liability rather than an asset.

Partly because more women than men reach old age, they are more often the victims of abuse and exploitation. It has been said that women tend to lose power as they age and men tend to gain it. This may be true until men, also, become dependent on someone else.

ABUSE

Being 76 years old wasn't much fun for Nelson. He had spent this day, like most every day, in the chair next to his bed. It had been over twelve hours since his daughter-in-law and son had come to check on him. He had soiled himself. He was also very hungry.

Nelson had lived with the couple since his stroke a year ago. Speaking clearly was difficult, and he found it easier to yell. When no one responded, he'd resort to swearing. When he swore at his daughter-in-law, she would became upset and slap him. Then, as punishment, she would leave him, sitting in his own urine and feces until his buttocks were raw. All he needed was to use the bathroom. Why did that make her so angry? Why didn't his son stop her? He felt so degraded, soiled like a baby.

Nelson shouted again. Finally, the door opened. His daughter-in-law knew that he had messed himself again and screamed obscenities. She towered over him, a prisoner in his chair, slapping his face and arms as hard as she could. Then she stormed out of the room, slamming the door behind her.

Nelson's loose flesh stung from her strikes. But what hurt most was that his son would believe her lies about his bruises.

"He fell out of bed, again," she would tell her husband. Nelson desperately wanted someone to help him, to take him out of this place, to care about him. But no one else ever came into his room. Even if they had, how could he tell them his own family treated him this way.

According to the Colorado Elder Abuse Prevention Program, Nelson's case, though inexcusable, is typical. The dynamics of elder mistreatment are readily recognized in Nelson's situation. They include:

- The victim is dependent on the abuser for basic survival needs.

- The victim may feel too embarrassed, or be unable to seek help.

- The victim's inability to control his own victimization lowers his self-esteem and increases his dependency and learned helplessness.

- The victim fears he will be abandoned or sent to a nursing home.

- The victim hopes that someone will rescue him and stop the abuse.

Poverty and isolation hide much elder mistreatment from public scrutiny. Many abused elderly are often members of dysfunctional families with a lifelong cycle of violence. Younger families who are struggling financially may be resentful of another mouth to feed. Sometimes, abusive behavior by family members is retribution for past abuses by the now dependent elderly person. Other abusive situations may arise as caregivers have exhausted their coping defenses.

Even professional care facilities, where employees work their shift then go home, are sometimes guilty of mistreating their patients. Forty percent of nursing home residents are victims of verbal abuse, and as much as 15 percent are victims of physical or sexual abuse.

It is estimated that in 1988 as many as two million elderly were deliberately hurt in some way by their caregivers. Elder abuse is a shocking testimony to our inability to cope with the physical, emotional, and financial demands of those who once cared for us.

Most victims are white women over the age of 75, who are in the custody of a family member because of some physical or mental disability. Statistics reveal sons are responsible for two-thirds of physical and emotional abuse.

Yet elder abuse is one of the least reported personal crimes. According to the Select Committee on Aging, only a fraction of incidents are ever brought to the attention of authorities. Victims who do report abuse have been accused of being senile, labeled chronic complainers, or are threatened with institutionalization. Some instances of abuse go undetected if the elderly person cannot communicate because of an organic brain dysfunction, such as Alzheimer's disease.

Like other forms of domestic violence, elder abuse doesn't happen only once. It's a cycle that becomes more frequent and more intense as time passes. Abuse isn't limited to hitting, slapping, and beating that result in broken limbs, bruises, sprains, or lacerations. Elder mistreatment can also take the form of sexual abuse, emotional abuse, unreasonable confinement, and over sedation. Because many of its victims are so frail, any form of elder abuse can be fatal.

The elderly experience a range of reactions to mistreatment similar to other victims of abuse. Individual personalities and the severity of abuse largely determine if the reaction will be passive withdrawal, or extreme anxiety that may lead to suicide. In between are states of confusion and disorientation, fearfulness, and helplessness.

Intervention is sometimes more difficult because the elderly are often confined, away from visitors and others who may find bruises and lacerations suspicious. Ironically, the abused elderly person may be protective of the abuser, especially if he or she is a son or daughter. They may also fear retaliation or institutionalization.

Protection of the victim, the primary goal of intervention, sometimes requires legal action. It is also important to help family members improve their coping skills through family-centered therapy.

Caregivers can assist elderly victims and their families in a number of other ways:

- Investigating acceptable placement options for elderly victims

- Linking them with local counseling services

- Helping them relieve stress by contacting support programs such as Meals on Wheels, hospice or respite care, nursing care, or shuttling services

- Teaching them interpersonal communication or transactional skills

From M. Quinn and S. Tomita's *Elder Abuse and Neglect,* are excerpted and abbreviated three potentially life-saving suggestions for elderly persons:

- Do not rely solely on family for your social life or for care if you have health problems. Continually cultivate friends of all ages so there are always people around who are genuinely concerned about you.

- If an adult child, particularly one who has led a troubled life, wants to return home to live with you, think it over carefully, especially if your family has a history of violent behavior or drug and alcohol abuse. Instead, consider supporting the child in his or her own apartment.

- If there has been alienation from family or friends, make peace to the extent possible, not only because it is the healing thing to do, but because it creates a climate of concern for you.

FINANCIAL EXPLOITATION

When Janice refused to put her mother in a nursing home, her husband, Bill, suggested they turn their son's old room into a comfortable suite for her. From the window, the aging woman could look out over the garden. Janice and Bill hired a nurse to stay with her throughout their workday. For a year, the arrangement seemed to work.

One Monday morning, the nurse didn't show up. Janice called her apartment and got no answer. Throughout the afternoon, Janice made phone calls. To her and Bill's shock, they learned the nurse had moved out of her apartment in the middle of the night.

That next week, Janice received her mother's bank statement. Four checks totaling $25,000 had been drawn against the account.

"It was all right to give her those checks, wasn't it?" her confused mother asked.

Financial exploitation means that the elderly, or anyone, has been illegally separated from their funds, property, or resources for another's profit or advantage. Surprisingly, the ones who should be protecting the interests of the elderly are exploiting them. More than two-thirds of abuse perpetrators are members of the victim's family. The remaining one-third are unscrupulous service providers, friends, and neighbors.

By some estimates, 20 percent of elder victimization involves financial exploitation. At greatest risk for scams and cons are those 65 or older who are physically or mentally impaired and dependent on a caregiver. Most victims of financial exploitation live on fixed incomes, often at or below poverty level. As a result, even a relatively minor loss creates a major impact.

Caregivers, friends, and family can identify possible financial abuse by looking for the following:

- Statements reflect unusual banking activity, drastic changes in withdrawals, or withdrawals from automated tellers inaccessible to the elderly person.

- The elderly person executes power of attorney, deed, or will when she no longer understands her financial situation.

- Individuals take unusual interest in the finances of the elderly person.

- Bills for living expenses are unpaid although someone other than the elderly person has been given that financial responsibility

- Recent acquaintances suddenly express gushy, pseudo-affection for the elderly individual.

- The elderly individual says he has signed papers or has visited an attorney but doesn't know why.

- The elderly person takes out a loan for no apparent reason.

- Checks or other documents are discovered that were not signed by the elderly individual.

To protect yourself or a loved one from financial abuse, talk with a trusted attorney, or call your local bar association for guidelines. Today's safeguards can prevent tomorrow's exploitation.

CRIME

Grocery shopping was always a Friday activity. For as long as she could remember, Bernice stocked up for the weekend. Now a widow living alone, she knew it was just a ritual, but it made her feel more secure.

As she carried her single grocery sack to the car, the strap of her shoulder bag slid to her elbow. She had noticed the Volkswagen beetle that crept slowly alongside her but thought it was merely anticipating her soon-to-be-vacant parking space. Suddenly its driver caught her off guard when he reached out and grabbed her purse.

Bernice dropped her groceries but kept her purse strap locked tightly on her arm. The beetle accelerated and yanked her to the ground. Before the strap broke, he had dragged her 100 feet. Her severely scraped body rolled into the curb.

Bernice spent several months in the hospital. Her injuries required multiple skin grafts and surgery on her knee. During and after hospitalization, she endured painful rehabilitation. She never regained her full mobility. Or her purse.

Purse-snatching in real life bears little resemblance to its television re-creation. Elderly victims, such as Bernice, unlike the younger victim left standing bewildered on the sidewalk, often suffer permanent disabilities as a result of injuries from a mugging.

To reduce the risk of loss or injury from muggings and purse- or wallet-snatching:

- Do not carry a large amount of cash, credit cards, or other valuables in your purse or wallet.

- Exchange your purse for a "fanny pack" and wear it securely around your waist, pouch turned to the front. Or carry your bag under your arm like a football and keep valuables in your pocket.

- Give up whatever the robber wants. Nothing you carry is worth injury or death.

- Walk in the middle of the sidewalk, facing traffic, not next to the curb where you are more vulnerable. Keep your distance from cars that slow down or stop to make inquiries.

Elderly victims can also suffer extensive psychological injury from crime. In the latter stages of life, the elderly often endure "chronic losses," which wear thin their emotional reserves: job; status; autonomy; death of family members and friends; income; health; even home. Physicians and mental health professionals have observed and documented the effects on body and mind of prolonged, or "chronic stress."

Robert Davis, former Director of Research and Information Systems for the Victim Services Agency in New York City, has brought the psychological toll of crime to the attention of the National Institute of Justice. Only recently, he says, have people come to realize that victims of crime "experience reactions similar to those experienced by victims of war, natural disasters and catastrophic illness."

Research on victims of crime, including the elderly, has provided the underpinnings for reforms designed to make the criminal justice system more responsive to the needs of older Americans. Its pivotal results have been to launch a movement toward greater victim involvement and to introduce legislation to create victim advocacy organizations. More than ever before, attention is being focused on coping styles, counseling techniques, and processes that help rather than hinder the victim's recovery from crime.

The criminal justice system has extended its concerns to include the special needs of elderly victims of crime for healing psychological as well as physical wounds.

The elderly generally react to crime in five ways:

- Their immediate reaction is shock and disbelief.

- They realize a greater sense of helplessness and, therefore, dependence. This is difficult for many elderly victims because they take pride in independence.

- They may feel incompetent and unable to function.

- They may feel worthless, devalued.

- Pride may prevent them from requesting financial compensation or other support.

RESPONDING TO THE ELDERLY VICTIM

The elderly do not want to be treated as children. They prize their autonomy and independence. Yet they need and want to know they are cared for. When victimization threatens their security and autonomy, family, friends, and professionals can be sensitive to their need to restore order and to feel competent that they will regain self-sufficiency.

Assure elderly victims that you are merely assisting while they get back on their feet. They are receiving help, not charity, during a difficult period. If their stress is compounded by financial need as a result of their victimization, talk with them about it. Professionals can make appropriate referrals to community services and victim compensation programs.

Avoid judgmental or accusatory statements such as, "Why didn't you lock your door? " or, "Why were you on the street after dark?"

Victims of crime should be encouraged to prosecute if their health and other life situations permit. They will need the ongoing support of friends, family and professionals during and after the criminal proceedings.

CHAPTER X

CHILDREN AS VICTIMS

Six-month-old Jessica arrived at the emergency room with a broken arm. Her mother said she had gotten it caught between the slats of her crib. Jessica looked familiar to the ER nurse. When she checked the hospital records, she wasn't surprised to learn that the baby had been treated for a broken leg only two months before. Informed of the second break, the physician ordered a full skeletal x-ray. On the light-box, he could see previous rib fractures that had healed.

The new information strongly suggested Jessica was a victim of child abuse. The physician notified law enforcement personnel and a protective hold was placed on the baby. The investigating officer had worked with enough cases of child abuse to recognize injuries inflicted by an adult.

Confronted with her daughter's other injuries, Jessica's mother began to cry. Now that authorities were placing her child in protective custody, she felt no need to lie.

A single mother, she had become involved with her current boyfriend when the baby was two months old. It had been a wonderful relief to have a man in her life. She soon discovered, however, that he became upset when the baby was fussy or cried. The first time he lost control, he grabbed Jessica around the chest and shook her violently. Her mother didn't realize that the baby's ribs were broken, even though Jessica cried for days every time she was picked up. Jessica's mother watched as her boyfriend took out his frustration on the baby. But she was afraid if she protected her helpless daughter, he would walk out on her. She couldn't stand to be alone again.

PHYSICAL ABUSE

Child abuse is the victimization through injury of any person under the age of 18 by someone else. The impact on defenseless children of neglect, physical, sexual, and emotional abuse can hardly be contained by the clinical word *victimization*. Clearly and simply, child abuse means an adult is out of control.

A child's innocence and inherent trust make him especially vulnerable to victimization. Like the elderly, the very young are powerless to prevent their exploitation. Because they cannot protect themselves, physical and sexual assault of the very young and the very old are particularly heinous crimes, evoking public compassion but little understanding of the short- and long-term suffering imbued in this type of victimization. There can be no doubt that neglect and physical, sexual, or emotional abuse take the child out of childhood. Unless the abuse is detected, reported, and the criminal prosecuted, the child is at risk for re-victimization.

We have labeled personality disorders, identified external factors that contribute to antisocial behavior, and are unraveling the mysteries of the human brain. Yet, for all its efforts, the scientific community still puzzles over morally and ethically acceptable ways to control violent behavior.

Protecting children is a social responsibility. Children may be abused as the result of poor parenting skills or overzealous discipline. In other instances, abuse is a malicious, or violent response by an adult to a child's misbehavior—*perceived* or *real*. More often than can be imagined, children suffer cruel torture.

Because infants and toddlers cry more and their needs place greater demands on their caregivers, they are commonly targeted for retaliatory abuse. Unable to cope with Jessica's normal baby fussiness, her abuser inflicted serious and repeated injury that—had she not been taken into protective custody—might have resulted in her death. Jessica's injuries were typical of babies her age. As a child grows older, he may receive "defense" injuries, bruises on hands and arms from blocking blows.

It is not unusual for a child in a home or school environment to be "targeted" and abused repeatedly by the same adult. The causes for such behavior are usually specific to the dynamics of the relationships in the setting where the abuse takes place. If the child is removed from that environment, the abuser may single out another child as a replacement target. For that reason, caregivers must always consider the safety of siblings or other children exposed to the abuser, even though there is no indication that they have been abused prior to intervention.

As in Jessica's case, the task of recognizing and reporting physical abuse has often been taken up by health-care professionals. Nevertheless, protecting children is everyone's responsibility. As protracted and severe stress permeates both the workplace and home, family members' inability to cope increases the potential that children will be subjected to, or targets of, explosive, life-threatening situations.

Intervening for the protection of the child must always be a first priority for caregivers, family, friends, and anyone who suspects the child is in danger of harm. For law enforcement personnel, it is justification for forcible entry. Although the mandate to report abuse exists in most states for teachers, therapists, clergy, medical personnel, and school personnel, we believe that protecting children is a moral obligation for everyone.

Each of us needs to be aware of physical indicators that a child is being abused. Generally, injuries are suspicious if they do not match the potential for the age and stage of development of the child. Physical indicators include:

- **Unexplained bruises.** These are usually in various stages of healing on the face, lips, or mouth, and on large areas on the torso, back, buttocks, or thighs. Bruises may also appear in clusters or regular patterns, mimicking the object used to inflict them, such as a belt buckle, or coat hanger.

- **Unexplained burns.** These include cigar or cigarette burns, especially on the soles of feet, palms of hands, back, or buttocks. Immersion, or "wet," burns include glove or sock-like burns around the hands and feet, and doughnut shaped burns on the buttocks or genitalia. Serious burns can occur within seconds when some part of the child's body is immersed into extremely hot water. Patterned, or "dry," burns show a clearly defined mark left by the instrument that inflicted them, such as an iron, electrical burner, or exposed electrical wires.

- **Unexplained fractures.** Although they occur most in children under the age of two, unexplained fractures that may result from child abuse cannot be ruled out in older children as well. When a child younger than two receives a fracture in a situation where the injury does not fit the developed abilities of the child, a skeletal x-ray is in order to determine if previous fractures exist. Multiple fractures in various stages of healing are a clear indicator of repeated abuse. Fractures of the skull, nose, facial structure, ribs, arms, legs, fingers, and toes normally trigger an investigation.

- **Unexplained brain trauma.** This trauma commonly occurs in infants as a result of severe shaking by a frustrated adult. Because an infant's brain does not fill the skull, severe shaking causes impact injury, bleeding, and swelling. Shaking often results in long-term or permanent damage, such as blindness, retardation, loss of motor skills, or learning disabilities.

- **Unexplained lacerations and abrasions.** Most common areas are mouth, lips, gums, eyes, external genitalia, backs of the arms, legs, and torso. Binding marks around the neck, ankles, and wrists may indicate the child was restrained in some manner.

- **Unexplained abdominal injuries.** Swelling of the abdomen, localized tenderness, and constant vomiting signal internal injury. Such injuries occur when a child is punched, kicked, or struck with an object in the abdomen or around the lower back in the area of the kidneys. These injuries are serious and can be fatal.

- **Human bite marks.** Abuse is usually signaled by recurrent, adult-size bite marks that may be found on any part of the body. Bite marks may also indicate sexual behaviors as well.

- **Deprivation of food, water, rest, or sleep.** These are a form of torture. Long-term, they can cause serious health problems or death.

A child whose world is no longer safe, who receives injury and pain when she behaves normally for her age, will make adaptations to alleviate as much pain and suffering as possible. Like a dog who has been repeatedly kicked and beaten, she will be wary of others, and apprehensive when she hears children cry. She may fight back, becoming increasingly aggressive or, conversely, overly-compliant. She may cry frequently or uncontrollably, show fear of her parents, or be afraid to go home.

SEXUAL ABUSE

Children do not seduce adults. Sex with a child, even a street-wise child, is a crime. So is *asking* a child for sex. There can be no consensual agreement between a child and an adult to engage in intercourse or any other sexual activity.

Yet, one in four girls and one in 10 boys will be sexually molested by age 18. Offenses can range from a single incident of exposure or fondling to years of repeated rape.

This illicit activity between an adult and child has been aptly labeled sexual *abuse* because the offender willfully exerts authority over the child, who lacks the physical and emotional maturity for self-protection. The molester sacrifices the child's well-being for self-gratification.

Child molesters can be males and females of all ages, races, religions, and socio-economic classes. They are heterosexual and homosexual. They may or may not be substance abusers, and most are not clinically insane. Any child is their potential victim.

Often without violence, the perpetrator subtly coerces the trusting child to engage in a variety of sexual activities—exposure of private areas to penetration of any bodily opening with a body part or foreign object.

Child sexual abuse, like rape, is a violation of power. Children who have been taught to trust and be obedient to adults are most easily violated. In approximately 75 percent of child sexual abuse cases, the perpetrator is a family member or friend of the family. His or her familiarity and authority coerce and ultimately engage the subordinate child in increasingly demanding sexual acts. The adult's leverage over the child enables him or her to control the frequency of sexual encounters as well as impose and maintain secrecy.

Perpetrators sometimes convince children that they were willing accomplices. The child who accepts this then adds guilt to an already heavy burden.

Sexually abused children are easily convinced that they have brought on the molestation. To assure their silence, perpetrators often threaten to hurt them, or someone or something they love or care about, such as a parent, sibling, or pet.

Because each child is emotionally unique, she or he will react to sexual abuse differently. It should be understood, however, that all child sexual abuse has the potential for a devastating outcome. On the short term, child victims have difficulty discerning whom to trust, or even that it is possible to trust anyone. In later years, they may have difficulty developing intimate relationships or these relationships may be fraught with sexual anxieties.

Children rarely make up lies about molestation. Most children realize that they have more to lose than to gain by a false accusation. Those who were molested while they were somewhere they shouldn't have been, or doing something they were told not to do, may be more fearful of being punished for breaking a rule than for revealing the abuse.

Tears streamed down Clarissa's pretty face. Her mother could scarcely believe her ears. Her 13-year-old daughter had inflicted a most painful blow. She knew it was true, but she didn't want to believe it. Now she realized the signs had been there all along. For two years! How could her husband have had intercourse with his daughter? It was beyond her ability to fathom. But there it was. Him barging in on her in the bathroom...emerging from her bedroom at 2 a.m.

"I hate it when Daddy comes into my room at night,"
Clarissa said. "I was just too afraid to tell anyone."

Had he threatened her if she told? Her mother loved them both, but she wouldn't see Clarissa's life ruined. Her husband had no right to molest his own flesh and blood. A mother had to protect her daughter.

When Clarissa's father came home from work, his wife confronted him. "I know you've been abusing Clarissa," she said without preface. She watched, emotionless, as he slumped onto the kitchen chair, his head cupped in his hands. She didn't want to hear his excuses, his promises that he would leave Clarissa alone. There was nothing more to say. Fighting back tears, she called the police. It seemed her whole world had been shattered.

Family and friends said she did the right thing. That's what she told Clarissa, too. "I know it was difficult for you, honey, but you did the right thing, telling me. We'll get through this, somehow. Your Daddy needs help. You won't have to be alone with him again."

We have seen that a child's understanding of sexual abuse and her prognosis for recovery are largely influenced by the actions of her parents or caregivers. The following are responses that are supportive of the child:

- Believe her. Let her know that telling you was the right thing to do.

- Let him know that you respect and understand his feelings. He may feel fearful, angry, embarrassed, guilty, or simply relieved.

- Assure him of your unconditional love.

- Assure her that she is not to blame. It is also important to explain that what happened to her was a crime and the abuser may go to jail.

- Assure him that you and others, such as friends and police officers, will protect and support him.

- Invite her to talk about what happened, when she is ready.

It didn't matter that Jody's father was a prominent banker and church elder. She was frightened of him. No. She hated him. He began touching her five years ago, when she was 10. He would come into her room when her mother wasn't home and put his penis in her mouth. Last night, when he forced his penis into her vagina for the first time, it hurt so bad. She really hated him.

When her mother got home, Jody told her. "Please, Mom, make him stop. Please, Mom."

But her mother only screamed at her and called her a slut. "Your boyfriend got you pregnant, didn't he? Isn't that why you're making up this horrible lie about your father? How can you say that? He'd never do such a thing."

Behind the closed door of her room—a place that held so many bitter memories—Jody cried. Mechanically, she stuffed T-shirts and jeans into her duffel. No one heard her slip out the back door to the safety of her girlfriend's house. She'd never step foot in her father's house again. He'd never touch her again. Ever.

Inappropriate responses confuse the child, leave him without support, and make recovery more difficult. Some examples of what not to do follow:

- Deny that abuse occurred

- Blame the child for the abuse

- Overreact, express anger at the child, or retaliation against the abuser

- Emphasize the child's victim status in front of him

- Overprotect the child by restricting normal, healthy activities

When a child is sexually or physically abused, he *and* his parents are victims. Many parents find it useful to seek help in resolving their feelings of anger, powerlessness, and guilt. Parents may also need to address the anxiety and inadequacy they feel in helping their child overcome the trauma.

It is not uncommon for parents of victims to have been sexually abused as children themselves. Remembrances of their own pain can open a Pandora's box of emotions. Sometimes parents who can successfully work through their own childhood trauma are better equipped to help their child overcome the effects of sexual abuse.

In the heat of the moment, parents who have discovered that their child has been sexually abused may convince themselves that confronting the molester is the right approach. Such confrontations, however, are not only potentially dangerous, but when they include assault, they are also unlawful. Further, they seriously undermine a wholesome parent-child relationship and give the child the wrong message about violence.

In addition to counseling, other strategies that can often help parents cope effectively with the crisis and take care of their own needs include:

- **Take time for themselves.** This can include time to read, visit a friend, or go some place enjoyable and relaxing. This time out teaches the child that everyone deserves time to himself. "Time out" isn't a rejection of others. It's an affirmation of self.

- **Keep a journal.** This can be a log of the events, appointments, interviews, and people involved in the case. It can also be a personal record of feelings. "Journaling" is a safe, creative, and valuable therapeutic tool.

- **Find a support group.** A safe place to ventilate feelings during stressful times can help prevent them from contributing to somatic, or physical, illness. Many communities offer support groups for parents of sexually abused children.

What Parents Can Expect

The effects of child sexual abuse vary widely from little or no apparent effect to devastating psychological and physiological harm. Their severity depends on a number of factors.

Research has shown that children suffer greater damage when the abuse is perpetrated by a family member over a long period of time. This is especially true when the child was controlled by secrecy and force.

Further, the experience of and the meaning to the child, as well as social conditioning, determine her response more than the acts themselves. A child who feels powerless, dirty, or guilty by the abuse, suffers greater trauma than the child who is unaware of being sexually abused.

The child's age may influence how he responds to the abuse. For example, the adolescent who knows that being touched in a sexual way by a friend or family member is wrong, yet unpreventable, may exhibit more trauma symptoms than a preschool child fondled by a relative who is otherwise caring and gentle.

It is not uncommon for children abused at a very young age to develop symptoms many years later as they become aware that what the abusive adult did was wrong.

A child's personal strengths and weaknesses also assist or hinder his emotional recovery. If he already suffers low self-esteem, perhaps as the result of family stresses, academic problems, or difficulties in making friends, he is more likely to interpret victimization as confirmation of his unworthiness. Conversely, if his self-image has evolved from a loving, supportive environment where he is a valued individual, he is less likely to be burdened by feelings of guilt and shame.

Parents attuned to their child's feelings and behaviors can detect subtle and, sometimes, not-so-subtle changes that signal guilt, anxiety, or depression.

Just as shame, guilt, and confusion are fodder for insecurity, these uncomfortable feelings may motivate the abused child to emotionally withdraw from family and friends. The insecurity can be compounded as she becomes overly sensitive to direction, discipline, and punishment. She may even burst into tears for seemingly no reason.

Sleep disturbances are common among sexually abused children. They may have trouble falling asleep or wake repeatedly in the middle of the night. As part of their subconscious coping strategies, they may revert to taking naps, going to bed early, or sleeping considerably longer than normal. Some children experience night terrors, reliving the trauma during sleep, or nightmares, terrifying dreams usually unrelated to the abuse.

Understandably, an emotional trauma that affects sleep and eating habits also affects performance at school. The pre-occupied child may lack concentration, become forgetful, and even aggressive. The usually well-behaved child who acts out angrily or with blatantly sexual gestures may be signaling for help.

Behavioral indicators that a child may have been sexually abused include:

- Sexual talk inappropriate for the child's age

- Bizarre, sophisticated, or unusual sexual overtures or knowledge

- Obsessive masturbation

- Poor peer relationships

- Discomfort with locker room exposure, participation in gym

- Delinquency or running away

Behavior changes are adaptations to emotional trauma over time. However, caregivers may observe immediate, physical symptoms of child sexual abuse that cannot be readily explained, such as headaches, vomiting, upset stomach, and hives. More specific indicators include:

- Difficulty in walking or sitting
- Torn, stained, or bloody underclothing
- Pain or itching in the genital area
- Frequency of, or difficulty in, urination
- Sexually transmitted disease
- Pregnancy

Official documentation of sexual abuse by medical professionals or law-enforcement officers relies, in part, on physical evidence that includes, but is not limited to: a perforated hymen; presence of the perpetrator's pubic hair, blood, or semen on the victim's mouth, genitalia, or clothing.

NEGLECT

It is not science fiction, or a futuristic, cinematic doomsday. It is reality. Here, now, in cities throughout the world, young scavengers raid dumpsters, pick pockets, sell their bodies, then curl up in sewers and condemned buildings to sleep the restless sleep of the dispossessed.

They are the blight on the fruit of economic progress. They are an error in judgment. A miscalculation. Neither education, technology, nor economic boom times explain their Dickinsonian existences away. Some exchange one inhospitable environment for another. Most have only each other and the streets.

Behind the closed doors of small suburban homes and fifth-floor tenements, hidden from the scrutiny of camcorders, are thousands of other children—abandoned and neglected—who lead lives of quiet desperation. Neglect hurts. Its territory is the pain of chronic hunger or unattended medical needs. It is the disenfranchisement from peers because of poor hygiene or inappropriate dress.

All week, Jason and Jerrad, 7 and 5, came to school in the same clothes. Their body odor was so strong that their teachers avoided getting close to them. Jason's teacher, Mrs. Russek, ushered the boys into the principal's office, then called social services.

A veteran social worker and a police officer drove the boys to their home in an affluent neighborhood. Their mother was upstairs, sprawled on her bed. Liquor bottles littered the floor, the night stand, the master bath. The room smelled like a distillery. Their mother had passed out again and had urinated on the bedspread. Vomitus crusted the expensive oriental rug.

Downstairs, the smell of rotting trash and dog feces permeated every room. The open kitchen cabinets held only a few cans of food. An empty jar of peanut butter rolled on the floor. In addition to their lunches at school, it was all the boys had eaten in the two weeks their mother drank herself into oblivion.

Jason had wanted to call their father in Newport, but they were afraid they'd get their mother in trouble.

"She already is," the social worker gently told him. Then she dialed the number of the alcohol treatment center.

Caregivers look for the following behavioral indicators of neglect or abandonment:

- Begging, stealing food

- Arriving early and departing late from school

- Chronic fatigue, listlessness, or falling asleep in class

- Alcohol or drug abuse

- Prostitution, theft, or other types of delinquency

- Chronically running away

It is difficult to understand why parents are neglectful. Statistics provide demographics and profiles such as mental retardation or low IQ, physical and financial incapacity to support and care for children, or substance abuse. Some parents are known to be so out of touch with reality that they cannot provide for their child's basic needs.

More commonly, however, neglectful parents are ordinary individuals with below-average self-esteem. They have few positive experiences in life, few successes and, perhaps, few skills. Often, they come from chaotic homes with poor role models. Even where alcohol and drugs are not involved, neglectful parents may be impulsive individuals who need and seek instant gratification without thought of its long-term consequences.

Caregivers and others who suspect neglect should immediately report the situation to a law-enforcement officer. In some states, with the exception of the courts, officers are the only parties with statutory authority to place a protective hold on a child.

EMOTIONAL ABUSE

The most subtle, elusive form of child abuse is emotional. We are a people of words. We have names for tangible and intangible things. Sometimes we use words to injure, hurling epithets or derogatory labels, knowing they will hit their mark.

How does one quantitatively measure the effects of words on a child? How do caregivers and professionals establish that emotional abuse slowly and painfully excises self-worth, chips away at self-image, and tears the child down?

Psychological research supports the theory that long-term, repetitive verbal assaults systematically devalue the importance of the individual. Rather than "waxing," the individual's personality begins "waning."

A child with long-term exposure to an unsupportive atmosphere reacts predictably. His behavior may range from compliant and passive to aggressive, or infantile to adult. The emotionally abused child may have trouble sleeping and may lose his appetite. In addition, he may develop speech disorders, or other physiological responses to the psychological distress.

Habit disorders, such as sucking, biting, or rocking, sometimes signal emotional abuse. In severe cases, he may become hysterical, or demonstrate obsessive-compulsive behavior, develop phobias or hypochondria. Dispirited and depleted, he may lose all interest in play and, if his parents wish him dead, he may attempt to accommodate their desire.

Emotional abuse comes in different packages. Some are marked "derogatory names" that label the child, perhaps for life, as a "misfit," "bastard," "idiot," "imbecile." Other packages are marked "unwanted," "unloved," "rejected," and leave the child in fear of abandonment. Still others deftly convey the message, "go away," or worse, "I wish you were dead."

Outside Thurston Elementary, Maria waited in the car for her six-year-old son. The bell rang. Suddenly, a sea of red, yellow, blue, and green dots flowed out of the building and dispersed into the sunlight.

Maria scanned the waves of children for Tony and spotted him near a tall woman whom she had seen before. Without warning the woman grabbed a small boy by the ear and yanked him in front of her.

"Look at me, stupid," she screeched. "I told you not to make me wait. I wish you had never been born."

Maria wanted to jump out of the car and comfort the trembling child. Still holding his ear, the woman dragged her terrified, embarrassed son to her car. Maria could still hear the horrible names she called him as they drove away.

The effects of emotional abuse—whatever form it takes—are cumulative and result in the annihilation of self and the destruction of the psyche. Eventually, a negative self-concept supplants a positive self-concept.

Parental Responses

Parenting is more than an act of conceiving and bearing children. To say the least, it is an awesome responsibility whose parameters are unconditional love, ceaseless energy, and enduring patience. Parenting is also about learned and intuitive skills and, of course, risk.

For most parents, defending offspring from predators is instinctual. From the dawn of time, preservation of the species has been programmed into our genes.

Humans take protection a step further, out of love and respect for the growing individuals who, in time, will be responsible for a whole new generation. They are not little adults, though they may look and behave something like us. They are evolving. As they learn the ways of the world, we hope to spare them pain and suffering, sheltered in our protective embrace.

But such idealism is removed from reality. Life is often cruelest to the most defenseless. Children *are* sometimes victimized by those they love and trust. Parents who discover that their child has been molested experience a range of emotions, beginning with anger. While a natural emotion, rage against the perpetrator doesn't address the child's need for support, which is essential for complete recovery of the whole person. This process largely depends on the responses of parents like you. It is appropriate to let the child know that you are angry, but emphasize that your anger is directed at the perpetrator, not at the child.

Emotional outbursts do not aid his healing process. Over-reaction merely spreads panic to the child. Because a child tends to blame himself for his parents' distress, he may withhold information simply to protect their feelings or to try to control their rage. Remain calm. Think rationally. Refrain from asking too many questions too soon.

IN COURT

Basic understanding of the legal process will help parents explain the coming events to their child. He will feel more secure if he knows what is about to happen and what may be expected of him. He will also feel better knowing his parents love and support him no matter how uncomfortable the proceedings may become for them.

Because the structure of the judicial system varies from state to state, parents and caregivers can ask their attorney or social services worker to explain procedures and keep them informed about the status of the case.

It may be helpful for your child to meet the prosecuting attorney before a hearing. He or she will establish a relationship with your child and will go over questions that may be asked at the hearing. Remind your child that it is safe to tell the truth.

The legal process can take in excess of one year to complete, which can prolong the trauma to the child and his family. Although the defense attorney will try to discredit witnesses for the prosecution and downplay the abuse incident, it is important to remember that it is the molester who is on trial, not the child.

Assure your child that he is loved and supported. Look not at the past, but to the future.

APPENDIX

As we have learned, there are many types of victims. Each has specific needs. Linking victims with the right help at the right time is an opportunity that caregivers and first-responders find particularly rewarding and gratifying.

The National Organization of Victim Assistance. NOVA, a non-profit organization, staffs a 24-hour hotline and acts as a clearinghouse for assistance information, crisis counseling and referral to victims, friends, family, and professionals.

NOVA conducts conferences and workshops, publishes information on victim rights and programs and offers organization membership. For information, write to NOVA, 717 D St., N.W., Washington, D.C. 20004. Information and referral services for people outside of Washington, D.C., is available by calling **1-800-TRY-NOVA**. Victims in the Washington, D.C., calling area can contact NOVA at **1-202-232-6682** for crisis counseling.

The National Victim Center, a nationwide, toll-free information and referral service, links victims to assistance programs and provides a valuable information hotline: **1-800-FYI-CALL.** Send written inquiries to: P.O. Box 17150, Fort Worth, TX 76102.

Many larger communities also have 24-hour hotlines. Check the white pages of your telephone directory for community services listings. These are usually found in the book's opening section and often include assistance and counseling information for specific types of crises.

Examples of the services that may be available are: **agency on aging, child abuse hotline, alternatives to family violence, suicide hotline, Legal Aid Society,** mental health services, rape counseling (assistance or awareness), parents' helpline, safe houses, senior services, Social Security Administration, substance abuse counseling, referral and support groups, half-way houses, emergency shelters for battered women, victim outreach services, and a runaway hotline.

Victims of violent crimes can obtain information about availability of a **Victim's Compensation Program** or **Victim's Assistance Program** in their state by contacting their local law-enforcement agency, district attorney's office, or prosecuting attorney's office.

Victims who were injured on the job as a result of a crime may be eligible for **Worker's Compensation** benefits. Their listing is often found in both the white pages and the special government section of the directory. **Social Security Administration** benefits may be available to qualifying individuals disabled by an injury received during a crime. The SSA listing can be found in the white pages under Social Security.

For information on first aid and CPR courses in your area, contact your local **National Safety Council** chapter, or the **National Safety Council First Aid Institute,** 1121 Spring Lake Drive, Itasca, IL 60143-3201, or dial **1-708-285-1121.**

FURTHER READING

Bard, Morton and Dawn Sangrey. *The Crime Victim's Book.* Basic Books, 1979.

Benedict, Helen. *Recovery: How to Survive Sexual Assault for Women, Men, Teenagers, Their Friends and Families. Rev. andexpandeded.* Columbia University Press, 1994.

Bohmer, Carol. *Sexual Assault on Campus : The Problem & the Solution.* Free Press, 1993.

Burgess, Ann W., editor. *Rape & Sexual Assault.* Garland Publishing, Incorporated, 1991.

Buzawa, Eve S. *Domestic Violence : The Criminal Justice Response.* Sage Publications, Incorporated, 1990.

Clark, David C., editor. *Clergy Response to Suicidal Persons & Their Family Members : An Interfaith Resource Book for Clergy & Congregations.* Exploration Press, 1993.

Copeland Lewis, Cynthia. *Teen Suicide : Too Young to Die.* Enslow Publishers, Incorporated, 1994.

Corry, Barbara. *Understanding Domestic Violence : A Recovery Resource for Battered Women & Those Who Work with Them.* Care Program, 1993.

Culligan, Joseph. *When in Doubt Check Him Out.* Hallmark Press, 1993.

Dvorchak, Robert. *Someone Stalking Me.* Dell Publishing Company, Incorporated, 1993.

Effects of Domestic Violence on Children. Gladden William, Foundation, 1994.

Farrington, Liz. *Exploring Grief.* Enchante Publishing, 1994.

Fattah, Ezzat A. *The Plight Of Crime Victims In Modern Society.* STMS, 1989.

Franks, D. *Help End Abusive Relationships (HEART) : A Personal Growth Program Manual for Battered & Formerly Battered Women.* Family Violence & Sexual Assault Institute, 1988.

Fritz, Barbara S. *Domestic Violence & Its Effect on Children.* Bureau For At-Risk Youth, 1992.

Geffner, R. *Child Physical Abuse-Neglect : A Categorized Bibliography & Reference List.* Family Violence & Sexual Assault Institute, 1992.

Geffner, R. *Elder-Parent Abuse : A Categorized Bibliography & Reference List.* -Family Violence and Sexual Assault Institute, 1992.

Geffner, R. *Sexual Abuse - Incest Survivors : A Categorized Bibliography & Reference List.* Family Violence & Sexual Assault Institute, 1992.

Geffner, R. *Spouse-Partner Abuse : A Categorized Bibliography & Reference List, updateded.* Family Violence & Sexual Assault Institute, 1992.

Goodman, Gail S. *Testifying in Criminal Court : Emotional Effects of Criminal Court Testimony on Child Sexual Assault Victims.* University of Chicago Press, 1992.

Goldman, Linda. *Life & Loss : A Guide to Help Grieving Children.* Accelerated Development, Incorporated, 1994.

Gunzberg, John C. *The Grief Counseling Casebook : A Student's Guide to Unresolved Grief.* Chapman & Hall, 1994.

Green, William M. *Rape: The Evidential Examination & Management of the Sexual Assault Survivor.* Free Press, 1988.

Greenberg. *Family Abuse.* Holt, Henry, & Company, Incorporated, 1994.

Greenberg, M. S. *After the Crime : Victim Decision Making.* Plenum Publishing Corporation, 1992.

Gregory, Howard. *Battered Husbands : The Battle of the Sexes Is Running Amuck.* Gregory, Howard, Associates, 1991.

Hartnett, Johnette. *Children & Grief, Vol. 5 : Big Issues for Little Hearts.* Good Mourning, 1993.

Helfer, Ray and Ruth Kempe. (Eds.) *The Battered Child.* University of Chicago Press, 1987.

Holinger, Paul C. *Suicide & Homicide Among Adolescents.* Guilford Publications, Incorporated, 1994.

Holmstrom, Lynda L. *The Victim of Rape : Institutional Reactions.* Transaction Publishers, 1991.

Hyde, Margaret. *Know about Abuse.* Walker and Company, 1992.

Johann, Sara L. *Domestic Abusers Terrorists in Our Homes.* Thomas, Charles C., Publisher, 1994.

Johnson, Scott. *When "I Love You" Turns Violent.* New Horizon Press, 1993.

Johnson, Tanya Fusco. *Elder Mistreatment: Deciding Who is at Risk.* 1991.

Kilgore, Nancy. *Every Eighteen Seconds : A Journey Through Domestic Violence. -- rev. ed.* Volcano Press, Incorporated, 1993.

Korbin, Jill E. (ed.). *Child Abuse & Neglect.* University of California Press, 1983.

Kuklin, Susan. *After A Suicide Young People Speak Up.* PUTP, 1994.

Kurland, Morton L. Coping with Family Violence. -- rev. ed. Rosen Publishing Group, Incorporated, 1990.

Ledray, Linda. *Recovering from Rape.* Holt, Henry, & Company, Incorporated, 1994.

169

Lester, David. *Patterns of Suicide & Homicide in America.* Nova Science Publishers, Incorporated, 1993.

Lein, Laura. *Property Crime Victims : An Analysis of Needs & Services* . Johnson, Lyndon B., School of Public Affairs, 1992

Lein, Laura. *Services for Crime Victims.* Johnson, Lyndon B., School of Public Affairs, 1991.

Lindquist, Scott. *Before He Takes You Out : The Safe Dating Guide for the 90's.* Vigal Publishers, 1989.

McEvoy, Alan. *Preventing Youth Suicide.* Learning Publications, Incorporated, 1994.

McIntosh, John L. *Elder Suicide: Research, Theory, & Treatment.* American Psychological Association, 1994.

Madigan, Lee and Nancy Gamble. *The Second Rape: Society's Continued Betrayal of the Victim..* Lexington Books, 1989.

Maguire, Mike, editor. *Victims of Crime A New Deal?.* Taylor and Francis, Incorporated, 1988.

Marecek, Mary. *Breaking Free from Partner Abuse : Voices of Battered Women Caught in the Cycle of Domestic Violence. -- rev. & enl. ed.* Morning Glory Press, Incorporated, 1993.

Martin, Laura. *Life Without Fear : A Guide to Preventing Sexual Assault.* Rutledge Hill Press, 1992.

Maxwell, Judith. *Full Circle : The Phase II Manual: A Support Group Guidebook for Battered Women.* Veda Vangarde Foundation, 1993.

Mitsch, Raymond R. *Grieving the Loss of Someone You Love.* Servant Publications, 1993.

Morgan, Jane. *Child Victims : Crime, Impact, & Criminal Justice.* Oxford University Press, Incorporated, 1992.

Muraskin, Roslyn. *It's a Crime : Women & Justice.* Prentice Hall, 1992.

NOVA Staff. *Victim Assistance : Frontiers & Fundamentals.* Kendall/Hunt Publishing Company, 1993.

Paymar, Michael. *Violent No More : Helping Men End Domestic Abuse.* Hunter House, Incorporated, 1993.

Poling, James N. *Abuse of Power : Theological Problem.* Abingdon Press, 1991

Quina, Kathryn. *Rape, Incest, and Sexual Harassment: A Guide for Helping Survivors.* Praeger, 1989.

Reed, Robert D. *Rape - Sexual Assault: How and Where to Find Facts and Get Help.* R & E Publishers, Incorporated, 1993.

Roberts, Albert R. *Helping Crime Victims : Research, Policy, and Practice.* Sage Publications, Incorporated, 1990.

Rudman, Jack. *Crime Victims' Advocate.* National Learning Corporation, 1991

Sank, Diane, editor. *To Be a Victim : Encounters with Crime & Injustice.* Plenum Publishing Corporation, 1991.

Santos, John F., editor. *Elders at Risk : Abstracts of the Psychological & Behavioral Literature on Elder Abuse, Victimization, & Suicide, 1967-1993.* American Psychological Association, 1993.

Shapiro, Ester R. *Grief as a Family Process.* Guilford Press, 1994.

Smith-Fliesher Soria, Sharon. *Closeted Screams : A Service Provider Handbook for Same-Sex Domestic Violence Issues.* Smith-Fliesher Soria Publishers, 1992.

Sosa, Roberto. *The Common Grief; Selected Poems.* CRBS, 1994.

Stringer, Gayle M. *So What's It to Me? : Sexual Assault Information for Guys.* King County Sexual Assault Resource Center, 1987.

Strommen. A. Irene. *Five Cries of Grief.* -- Harper San Francisco, 1993.

Talley, Jim. *My Father's Love*. Nelson, Thomas, Publishers, 1992.

Victims of Child Abuse; Domestic Violence; Elderly Abuse; Rape, Robbery, Assault; & Violent Death : A Manual for Clergy & Congregations. Diane Publishing Company, 1992.

Volkan, Vamik D. *Life after Loss : The Lessons of Grief*. Macmillan Publishing Company, Incorporated, 1993.

Webster, Linda, editor. *Sexual Assault & Child Sexual Abuse : A National Directory of Victim Services & Prevention Programs*. Oryx Press, 1989.

Wittet, Scott. *Helping Your Child Be Safe*. King County Sexual Assault Resource Center, 1987.

Wolf, Rosalie S. and Karl A. Pillemer. *Helping Elderly Victims*. Columbia University Press, 1989.

Wood, Wendy and Leslie Hatton. *Triumph Over Darkness*. Beyond Words Publishing, 1989.

Wright, Martin. *Justice for Victims & Offenders : A Restorative Response to Crime*. Taylor & Francis, Incorporated, 1991.

Wrobleski, Adina. *Suicide Survivors: A Guide For Those Left Behind*. Afterwords Publishing, 1991.

Zagdanski, Doris. *How teenagers cope with Grief : Something I've Never Felt Before*. Seven Hills Book Distributors, 1994.

SURVIVING: A Guide for Victims, Families, Friends, and Professionals

About the Authors

Allison Brittsan, M.A., has been helping victims for more than 10 years. In 1989 she was named "Victim Advocate of the Year" by the Colorado Organization of Victim Assistance. As a workshop and seminar presenter, she is frequently called upon to teach first-responders effective responses to victimization. In her private practice she specializes in trauma recovery. She is co-author of *Sexual Assault of Children: A Parent's Guide,* and co-editor of *Assisting Victims and Survivors: A Police Officer's Guide.*

Lt. Clarene Shelley, M.A., conducts workshops, seminars and training sessions for law-enforcement personnel and other professionals in responses to victimization, with special emphasis on child abuse and sexual assault. Lieutenant Shelley, currently with the Lakewood, Colorado, Police Department, has more than 20 years of law-enforcement training and supervisory experience. She is co-editor of *Assisting Victims and Survivors: A Police Officer's Guide.*